Creative Politics

Creative Politics

Taxes and Public Goods in a Federal System

GLENN BEAMER

Ann Arbor

THE UNIVERSITY OF MICHIGAN PRESS

First paperback edition 2000
Copyright © by the University of Michigan 1999
All rights reserved
Published in the United States of America by
The University of Michigan Press
Manufactured in the United States of America
⊗ Printed on acid-free paper

2002   2001   2000   4   3   2

A CIP catalog record for this book is available from the British Library.

Library of Congress Cataloging-in-Publication Data

Beamer, Glenn, 1966–
    Creative politics : taxes and public goods in a federal system /
Glenn Beamer.
        p.   cm.
    Includes bibliographical references and index.
    ISBN 0-472-11020-9 (cloth : alk. paper)
        1. Taxation—United States—States.   2. Federal government—United
States.   3. Finance, Public—United States—States.   I. Title.
HJ2053.A1   B4   1999
336.2′00973—dc21   98-58121
                                                                CIP

ISBN 0-472-08730-4 (pbk. : alk. paper)

To the memory of my grandfather,

Louie Wyman Rehberg

January 12, 1911
Thomasville, Georgia

February 21, 1990
Allentown, Pennsylvania

Contents

Acknowledgments

Many people have contributed to this book, and I am grateful to all of them. I thank the scores of state legislators who freely gave their time and provided the thoughtful insights that form the basis for this book. Because of our initial agreement, they will remain anonymous, but my debt to them is great, and many of them went far beyond the call of civic duty to assist me. I am also grateful to the many staffers, lobbyists, and state political activists who took an interest in my work and helped me find valuable evidence to corroborate what the legislators were saying and helped accommodate my work in their capitals.

This work began at the University of Michigan in 1994. I am most grateful to Nancy Burns, who served as my dissertation director and has contributed greatly to this book. Nancy facilitated my research, always supported my field endeavors, and encouraged me to focus the work and develop reasonable arguments. I also thank Ken Goldstein for his often prescient advice and counsel as this project has developed over the past four years.

John Kingdon assisted me tremendously in preparing for the fieldwork and in channeling the analyses of collective decision making. I am also indebted to John for providing guidance on presenting comparative case studies of state politics and on how to best use the interviews. John Huber helped me to focus on comparing legislatures and using the case evidence to draw sound conclusions about collective decisions. Paul Courant and Sheldon Danziger helped me develop my thinking about the interactions among public goods and politics. Grace York at the Graduate Library in Ann Arbor provided tremendous help in developing documentation and background materials for the case studies. Finally, I benefited greatly from comments and suggestions from Kent Jennings, Susan Ellis, and Mel Laracy during our collegial seminar in 1994. Without their help, I might still be staring at a blank computer screen.

At the University of Virginia, I am grateful to David Waldner for conversations regarding comparative case studies. I am also grateful to Steve Finkel for his support while I was reworking the manuscript during my two eventful, often fun, years in Charlottesville. Paula McClain and Robert Fatton were supportive throughout and made every effort to facilitate the completion of this project. Alice Ba carefully read and critiqued the entire manuscript, and I am grateful to her. Michael Zlatoper provided valuable feedback on chapter 5, and Scott Horlacher helped me revise chapter 7.

At the University of Michigan Press, Chuck Myers, Kevin Rennells, and Stephanie Werhane have all been very helpful. I appreciate their cooperation, guidance, and assistance in revising and preparing this manuscript.

This book was completed while I was a Robert Wood Johnson Scholar in Health Policy Research at the University of California at Berkeley. I am particularly grateful to Allen Cohen, Eileen Conner, and Richard Scheffler for supporting this project. I am indebted to Tim Prinz for general comments about the manuscript and specific comments about chapter 7.

This research has received financial support from several sources. At the University of Michigan, I was privileged to receive a Gerald R. Ford Dissertation Fellowship and Research Grant from the Department of Political Science. I also received a Dissertation Research Grant and a Rackham Research Partnership with Nancy Burns from the Rackham Graduate School at the University of Michigan. Sheldon Danziger supported various projects, all of which facilitated progress. At the University of Virginia, I received a Rowland Egger Small Grant, which helped me complete the manuscript. The Robert Wood Johnson Scholarship provided valuable time and resources with which to make final revisions to the manuscript.

All of these people have contributed much to this book, and I am in their debt. Any errors are entirely my responsibility.

This book is dedicated to the memory of my grandfather, Louie Rehberg. Next to his family, he most enjoyed politics, and he was my first teacher in the field. I thought of him often and fondly in conducting the field research for this book.

Chapter 1

Federalism as Creative Politics

Assembly Member: You should have been here last week, Glenn, if
you wanted to learn how we create revenue policy in New York.
One of my environmentalist friends made a statement about our
nickel deposits on bottles and how great this was. So then, I don't
know, Smedlap stands up and says, "Hey, what happens to the
deposits nobody claims?" Good question, and it turns out none of
us knew, so of course a third guy gets up and says, "Let's have the
vendors remit their unclaimed deposits to the state. It'll be a revenue source." So then I get up and say, "If you're gonna do that,
let's make it a dime," like I believe you have in Michigan. And then
I get one-upped by someone who says, "We pay a buck for a coke
in the city, so let's make the deposit a quarter," and to that this
Republican from out on the island says, "At that sort of a deposit
welfare mothers will be out getting bottles to bring in and make
cash income so we ought to cut the AFDC grant if we're going to do
it," and he says, "Now we've got a jobs program here." Then a
Democrat gets up and says, "If we must cut spending on welfare,
then we must get some real money out of the bottle scam . . . so let's
make the deposits a dollar," and then another guy screams, "A
buck—you make it a buck, and it's so lucrative not only will there
be no unremitted deposits, but the mafia will be driving over to
Pennsylvania (where there's no deposit) and collecting all the bottles and drinking all the soda they can to ring the state dry on our
buck-per-bottle law." It was outrageous.

GB: So what happened?

Assembly Member: Well, once you mention the Mafia—one of my colleagues got up and said we were defaming Italians, so we dropped
the whole thing. Hey, I'm Italian, I loved it—that's how we work
around here. I love it, only in New York, pal.

This illustration, although humorous, illustrates quite a bit about the spirit of federal politics. The legislator's comments reveal the state government's need, apparently dire, for obscure revenue sources. The recycling program itself indicates legislators' concerns about providing a public good such as a cleaner environment. The comments about Michigan indicate an awareness of policy diffusion among states. The comments about the connections between recycling and welfare and jobs programs reveal elected officials' policy linkages, which can be creative. Finally, the comments about Pennsylvania's lack of a "bottle bill" indicate New Yorkers' worries that although a policy might initially appear good for the Empire State, its interaction with other states' policies, or lack thereof, could portend unintended negative consequences.

This book asks two questions central to the understanding of federal politics and political representation in federal systems. First, how do relationships among political institutions alter the politics and collective decisions that involve cooperative or competitive endeavors among different governments? Second, how does the public sector's responsibility for the provision of nonexclusionary public goods—from clean air to roads to education to health services—change federal politics?

Federalism changes politics. The structures and arrangements among political institutions change the incentives and constraints individual politicians face when developing public policy (Chubb 1985). Yet few scholars have investigated how elected representatives respond to these objective, or structural, changes in policy parameters. On a more subjective level, federalism changes the issues politicians face and the views voters hold about various programs and policies. National politics spill into state politics. Local politics bubble up to the state level, forcing state legislators to contend with issues they had not foreseen or sought and sometimes do not welcome.

Federalism changes politics within political institutions. Federal financing, funding formulas, regulations, and court rulings influence from above the agendas and collective decisions of state legislatures. From below, demands from and the resource limits of municipalities and local governments alter the agendas and decisions made by locally elected state representatives. Legislatures may consider a response but fail to agree on an alternative; they may agree on a response that only symbolically addresses a problem emanating from another level of government; or they may attempt to act only to find changing national or local politics preclude their responses. Sometimes, however, the legislature and other state elected officials will agree on a major policy alternative as a response and enact it, as Michigan did with education finance reform or Tennessee did with Medicaid.

Scholars (Peterson 1981; Chubb 1985) have presented models of federalism focusing on the structures and purposes of federalism. Although these models describe the structure of federal politics and the purposes of federal policies, they provide less information about how actors in political institutions view federal politics on a day-to-day basis and about how elected representatives use the avenues federalism creates. I present a model that offers important new insights into how intergovernmental relationships create and change politics, how the structural relationships among governments influence elected officials' thinking about policy alternatives, and how these changes in thinking affect both the politics observed and the policies governments produce. I also consider how legislators' views about the scope of program benefits, their inclusiveness in providing public benefits, and their responses to incentives to assist particular constituencies translate into collective decisions to determine mixes of public goods, particular benefits, and tax systems.

Federal politics are creative politics. The structural arrangements among governments and the more informal, often competitive, relationships among subnational governments create new politics that would not exist in centralized or unitary governments. Institutional arrangements allow for debates about how to provide goods and services, and federalism frames these debates differently than would centralized or unitary governments. The relationships among governments create competitions not just across equivalent governments but among government levels, as elected officials claim credit for popular programs, shift blame for unpopular policies, and avoid responsibility for financing them with taxes.

Federalism changes the provision of public goods by creating a desire among officeholders to claim credit for programs and their benefits and to avoid responsibility for imposing taxes. These incentives and constraints frame several questions for political science. How do representatives define public goods? How do elected representatives decide which government should provide which goods, how should these goods be financed, and how should benefits flow? The critical point about public goods is that they are nonexclusionary. In federal systems, the nonexclusive nature of public goods complicates governing because elected officials seek credit for the benefits from public goods while avoiding responsibility for the taxes that finance them. Also, subnational elected representatives attempt to exclude their public-goods' benefits from citizens outside their jurisdictions yet are only too happy to export the tax burdens necessary to finance these goods.

Economists have paid considerable attention to public goods (Samuelson 1954; Buchanan 1968). Because demand for public goods is derived differently than demand for private or exclusionary goods, governments better provide an economically efficient level of public goods than do private markets (Gramlich 1990). But economists have not investigated how public goods "firms"—governments and their ostensible managers, elected officials—approach their task. What do politicians consider exclusionary goods best provided privately and what do they consider public goods? Many government programs provide benefits that are neither strictly private goods nor public, nonexclusionary goods. Thus a good deal of gray area exists inside and outside legislative chambers about what government should provide and how.

State legislators spend considerable time determining, debating, and evaluating the prices and price systems for both public goods and particular benefits programs. These price systems are taxes. State legislators spend considerable energy discerning whether the public will accept these price (tax) systems and attempting to connect specific taxes with specific government programs and benefits.

To understand how federal structural arrangements and the nonexclusionary nature of public goods change subnational politics, I focus on the collective decisions of legislatures in four policy areas—taxes, economic development, education finance, and Medicaid.

Taxes are fundamental to government operations of any sort (Levi 1987). All state governments face the same federal tax system and its structural constraints and incentives, yet a great deal of variance persists among state tax systems and the changes in them during the 1990s. Also, states create localities and in many cases design and shape local tax parameters. The relationship of state systems to the federal system and states' responsibility for defining local tax options, if not the tax systems themselves, offer substantial reasons to investigate how states respond to national and local tax politics.

Economic development efforts have become a second universal among the states, and these efforts illustrate the horizontal competition that has developed in the U.S. federal system (Eisinger 1988; Peterson 1981; Dye 1990). While scholars have done much to identify policies and estimate their efficacy, I examine them to illustrate how state legislatures can choose either a "public goods" or a "particular benefits" approach to achieve the same outcome—an improved economy.

The later chapters focus on education financing and health care, respectively. These policy contrasts illustrate several points germane to the investigation of how institutional arrangements and perceptions about public goods create subnational politics and influence policy choices. In the case of education, legislators sought to change financing to preserve public support for a program, primary and secondary education, they perceived as having broad political support at both the elite and mass levels. In the case of Medicaid, legislators sought to fix inequities in the exclusive nature of the program (i.e., providing benefits only to unemployed parents and their dependents) and to incrementally reestablish general support for public-health programs. Also, the chapter on education financing investigates fiscal and political arrangements between states and localities. The Medicaid chapter presents an analysis of interactions between states and the federal government.

Although the primary units of analysis are the legislatures' collective decisions, I present considerable data about representatives' individual positions and policy preferences. I do so to establish a better foundation for understanding the legislatures' collective decisions and to offer readers a means to see how individual positions mapped onto the collective decisions and how those positions were translated via the policy process.

With respect to legislators' positions for specific policy alternatives, I attempted to determine the legislators' ideal policies for any given issue and then sought explanations as to why each legislator supported one viable alternative over another. What principles guide state legislators' decisions about financing their governments? How does federalism affect state politics and policies? These governing principles and positions provide the foundation for understanding legislatures' policy decisions.

After establishing both the policy background and the explanations legislators offered for their individual positions, I turn to the primary unit of analysis—the collective policy decisions of legislatures. Legislators perceptions of the program, their governing principles, and their responses to intergovernmental politics interacted with institutional politics, their state constitutions, policy histories, and opportunities for citizen and interest-group influence on the policy process to produce the policy changes and failed attempts at policy changes on which I focus in the policy chapters.

Research Methods

To acquire adequate data on legislators' individual positions and their collective decisions, I conducted case studies of eleven state legislatures during 1994 and 1995. The issues with which I was concerned included taxes, economic development, education, and health care. I consider a case to be a "state issue." I consider all of the states dealing with tax policy and economic development in chapters 4 and 5. In chapter 6, which examines school financing, I present cases from Massachusetts, Vermont, New Jersey, Michigan, Mississippi, Colorado, and Oregon. To a lesser extent I provide supporting information about school finance from New York and Florida, although in neither state was school finance reform a central issue. I examine Florida, Tennessee, Vermont, Washington, Oregon, and Colorado in chapter 7, which deals with health care and Medicaid.

I conducted open-ended interviews with 123 state legislators. In addition, I interviewed several dozen legislative staffers, state lobbyists, local officials, and political activists. The interviews focused on taxes in every state and to varying degrees on education financing, economic development, health care, and government mandates. The interviews yielded an understanding of legislators perceptions about both their representative roles in the federal system and their individual positions on various state policies particularly germane to the interest in federal politics. The interviews collectively explained policy outcomes and decisions in specific states for specific issues.

Representatives acted as informants for decisions their legislatures either made or were in the process of making from 1992 through 1994. Based on the initial criteria that a state consider changing its income, sales, business, or property taxes during that period, nineteen states were considered as potential case-study states. I selected eleven to provide geographic and political variance in the cases as well as the capability of investigating different outcomes in the process.

Had I focused on a single state or case, the interviews with legislators might have been more numerous within a single state, but I could not have generalized about legislatures' collective decisions. By using a range of cases and by collecting both primary and secondary evidence, I offer an analysis with greater external validity.

By going to the states, I achieved far more depth using interviews and primary-source data collection than aggregated outcome data allows. The interviews demonstrated the consistent presence of the six governing principles outlined in chapter 3. To corroborate the interview data, I collected materials to confirm and contrast the information supplied by the legislators. These sources included interviews with lobbyists, staff, and journalists as well as source documents such as bills, committee reports, administrative memoranda, and budget briefings.

The case studies strengthen the assessment of the relationship between federalism and legislators' positions, and they illuminate how federalism and public goods change legislatures' collective decisions. By conducting individual interviews, I could better ascertain a legislator's most preferred policy and contrast it with the policy alternatives considered by a legislature or the final roll-call vote on a single alternative. Moreover, I can estimate a spectrum of possible positions and ideal policy preferences among legislators across states for different policies. Roll-call analyses would not provide this latitude.

With respect to the generalizability of the case studies, I have provided sufficient breadth with respect to who was interviewed and among the fifty states to conclude that the basic principles and politics observed can be generalized beyond the specific cases. Legislators' emphasis among the principles they use in formulating positions and in responding to federal-state and state-local policy proposals comport across several states for any given issue and across the issue areas. For example, concerns about revenue dependability surfaced in discussions about taxes, Medicaid reform, and local school financing.[1] Readers with an interest in the case-study methodology may wish to read appendix A.

Overview

In the next chapter, I present a model of representation embedded in federalism that explicitly incorporates the nonexclusionary nature of public goods in the representation calculus. This model enables the understanding both of how relationships among governments influence representatives' thinking and of how the nonexclusionary nature of public goods leads to variations in state politics and federal policies. I elaborate on the independent variables, the structure and relationships produced by federalism and the nature of public goods, and the dependent variables—legislatures' collective decisions about their own programs that affect and are affected by other governments' programs and their decisions about intergovernmental programs.

In chapter 3, I outline representatives' individual governing principles, which are invoked in deciding which policy alternative to support and how to explain that decision. Representatives emphasized different principles for different issues and placed varying amounts of emphasis on the various principles across issues and states.

Beyond chapter 3, I examine different policy issues confronting state representatives and analyze how different principles and political contexts have led to different outcomes. I have attempted to present a fairly complete picture of each policy and its representation consequences among states without presenting so many details as to make comparisons unwieldy. In chapters 4 and 5, I examine state tax and development efforts, which offer insights into the competitions among states as well as the most basic of public-goods positions (the income-distribution and tax burdens) within the case states.

In chapter 4, "Read Our Lips: No New (Income) Taxes," I discuss the symbolism of federal income taxes and how citizens' disdain for those taxes has constrained legislators' efforts to enact state income taxes even when legislators perceive income taxes to provide the most appropriate means of funding state programs. This chapter demonstrates that in addition to the structural relationships among government, politics flow and citizen responses to policy changes at one level of government affect the politics and policy alternatives for a second level.

In chapter 5, "Tax and Spend or Spending Taxes—Economic Development Policy," I examine the differences among states in pursuing economic development. Many states offer tax incentives to potential employers, but the substance of these incentives and who bears their costs vary. Other states emphasize providing public goods such as roads and education to foster economic development. Consequently, comparing state strategies offers insights into how federalism generally shapes subnational politics, and, more specifically, how the politics of providing public goods shapes economic development policy choices.

In chapter 6, I consider state and local representation trade-offs by examining education financing in Vermont, Michigan, Oregon, New Jersey, Mississippi, and Massachusetts. Many state representatives have supported assumptions of funding responsibility for primary and secondary education because of inequities in local tax bases, a perceived regressivity in property taxes, and their conviction that the state could better access and distribute funds than could localities. This chapter illustrates that legislators use federalism not simply to shift costs, claim credit, and avoid blame. They endeavor equitably to finance and produce services for their constituents. Several factors limit legislators' choices about which taxes to enact when assuming a local responsibility. The linkages as a state-local issue and the differences in how a public good is provided matter, as do constitutional definitions and representatives' perceptions about public goods and how to finance them.

Chapter 7 shifts the focus to national-state representation, with an examination of Medicaid policy. I draw on interviews from Tennessee, Florida, Colorado, Oregon, Vermont, and Washington to discuss how legislators worked to resolve their states' Medicaid crises, save state dollars, and provide more equitable health-care coverage for low-income individuals. The failure of Medicaid to retain political support coupled with the escalating cost of the program forced Democrats and Republicans to find ways both to save money and to broaden the distribution of benefits. In several states, these changes involved altering the benefits offered from reimbursements for health services rendered to state subsidies for insurance policies or health-maintenance organization memberships.

In chapter 8, I synthesize the evidence from the previous chapters to present a picture of representation in a modern federal system.[2] I analyze the differences in policy alternatives and outcomes across the four issues considered in chapters 4 through 7, and I consider how the different political and institutional aspects of each state influenced the differences observed across states. I find that public goods are indeed an important element of federal politics and that much of these politics center on the variance among legislators about what policy areas provide public goods and how governments should best provide them.

The conclusions illustrate that federalism should be studied from the perspective of subnational as well as national governments. To predict responses to national initiatives, it is necessary to understand how different political, economic, and financial contexts shape subnational representatives' responses. Once these contexts are understood, it is easier to predict the range of responses likely for a given national policy initiative. To make such predictions, it is important to understand that the most nebulous areas for legislators at any level of government involve policy in which both taxes and services either increase or decrease together. Most legislators know that increasing taxes and cutting services will evoke a negative response from voters, while decreasing taxes and increasing services will evoke a positive response. The difficulty for legislators transpires when they face choices in which services and taxes shift concomitantly and in the same direction. Chapter 2 provides a detailed consideration of this metric of policy change and representation, along with detailed discussions outlining the avenues of politics created by the incentives and constraints in federal arrangements and the role of public goods in federal systems.

Chapter 2

Federalism, Public Goods, and Taxes

One element of modern representation consists of representatives responding to their constituents' preferences for goods and services (Jewell 1982; Pitkin 1967). Responding to constituents' preferences is at best an uncertain undertaking. Citizens may not communicate their preferences well. There may be competing preferences from citizens within a legislative district. And citizens may be uncertain about their preferences or hold contradictory preferences (Jackson and Kingdon 1992). Pitkin (1967) has argued that representation is a process and posits an ongoing relationship between the representative and the represented. Representation involves responding to constituent demands for goods and services, not just in the narrow sense of pork-barrel projects but also in the broader sense of providing goods and services in accord with citizens' preferences and having governments impose tax systems citizens accept. An essential component of satisfying constituent preferences for government goods and services involves attaching appropriate pricing systems—taxes—to those services (see Levi 1987).

Krehbiel (1991) and Jewell (1982) offer insight into how legislators use information to shape their decisions about how to extract tax revenues and allocate benefits. Both scholars contend that legislators are more concerned with a broad-based allocation of tax burdens and resources than with particular benefits for their districts. Jewell examines the positions of individual legislators and does not examine cases in which legislators must collectively decide on an alternative. The second unit of analysis in this work, the collective decisions of the legislature, enables the extension of Jewell's work on state legislators to understand how individual positions translate into collective policy outcomes.

Of course, legislators respond to more than simple calculations about citizens' benefit/tax ratios. They must consider how policy changes affect various elements of the constituencies and the extent to which policy changes may mobilize support or opposition among interest groups, which can in turn offer substantial financial support for officeholders (Denzau and Munger 1986). Thus, calculations about service benefits and tax costs become two components in individual legislators' assessments of policy alternatives and the amount of political capital to commit beyond voting for or against a specific proposal.

Federalism and public goods also become components in legislators' policy decisions. If a legislature can shift costs onto another level of government or provide benefits to a broader range of constituents without increasing their costs, then representatives may seek new marginal revenues in response to intergovernmental programs and to the nature of public goods.

The federalism–public goods model of representatives' responsiveness complements other models of state policy development (Dye 1990; Erikson, Wright, and McIver 1993) by reflecting institutional political processes in the states. Legislators consider various issues, arrive at positions, and work toward policy outcomes in and around their legislative chambers. This model focuses on decision makers and collective policy decisions in federal political institutions rather than on the aggregate data for national and subnational jurisdictions. Examining the legislatures and legislative policy alternatives at the state level opens the black box of subnational institutions—they become an understandable component in the political process, and it is possible to unravel what happens and why.

As a metric for understanding resource allocations in federal systems, I employ the concept of a benefit/tax ratio (Peterson 1981). For an individual citizen, the benefit/tax ratio is the willingness to pay for a bundle of government goods and services divided by that individual's tax burden. The numerators and denominators can be aggregated across citizens to estimate a benefit/tax ratio for any community, legislative district, state, or nation.

Estimating benefit/tax ratios is at best an uncertain enterprise because citizens have incentives to understate their willingness to pay for public goods (Samuelson 1954; Tiebout 1956). It is possible, however, to discuss with some certainty what happens to benefit/tax ratios when legislatures enact policy changes. Because state legislators do not create an entirely new set of goods and services every session, attention can be focused on how policy changes affect various constituencies. When legislators increase tax rates only to maintain services, one can conclude that benefit/tax ratios have decreased. However, selecting certain citizens to bear additional taxes while maintaining services may maintain or even increase constituents' benefit/tax ratios. These changes in values can be estimated for individual citizens, for a district or group of legislative districts (e.g., those held by Democrats), or for an entire state.

Table 1 depicts the broad policy choices legislators make and the effects of those choices on benefit/tax ratios. Legislators can increase, decrease, or maintain taxes and services. When legislators increase taxes and cut services, benefit/tax ratios decline. When they cut taxes and increase services, benefit/tax ratios increase. Only when taxes and services are both reduced or increased concomitantly is there uncertainty about changes in citizens' benefit/tax ratios.

The cells in table 1 indicate the effect on benefit/tax ratios for various changes in state taxes and services. In three of the scenarios, benefit/tax ratios increase, and in three others they decrease. Benefit/tax ratios remain constant if neither services nor taxes change. Only when services and taxes both increase or decrease is there uncertainty over what happens to aggregate benefit/tax ratios. In an ideal world, legislators would prefer to deal with the three cells in the upper right corner of the table, which indicate increases in benefit/tax ratios, and would like to avoid confronting the three cells in the lower left corner, which show decreasing benefit/tax ratios.[1]

When taxes and service levels move together (i.e., the cells with question marks), collective choices may be shaped by the political resources available to legislators from affected interests and by the distributional effects a policy change produces. The political resources include votes, campaign contributions (financial and volunteer), and media; these resources in turn may be enhanced or constrained by factors such as the state's policy history, state constitutional limits on policy changes, and

TABLE 1.   Changes in Government Services, Taxes, and Benefit/Tax Ratio Changes

Services	Taxes		
	Increase	No Change	Decrease
Increase	?	Increase	Increase
No Change	Decrease	No Change	Increase
Decrease	Decrease	Decrease	?

opportunities for citizen participation in the policy process. The distributional effects depend on the economic or demographic profile of a representative's district, and these effects may lead legislators to shift either the burdens of a policy change (by altering a proposal) or the level of government responsible for it. These distributional considerations may encourage legislators to obscure the effects of the policy change.

One can interpret table 1 in terms of the overall effects of policy changes on citizens in a state or in terms of an individual citizen's benefit/tax changes. In the case of the former, a benefit/tax ratio may increase in the aggregate for a legislative district, but it need not do so for all citizens in that district. Legislators develop and enact policies with various effects for different citizens. For example, an increase in the income tax personal exemption might offset an increase in income tax rates. Consequently, while benefit/tax ratios decrease overall and most citizens pay higher taxes, some lower-income citizens may realize increases in their benefit/tax ratios as their tax burdens decrease.

In most policy decisions, and particularly for tax policy decisions, legislators face questions about not only the aggregate effects but also the distributional effects on their districts and individual constituents. How can the benefits and costs of a program be dispersed? Who should pay higher taxes in return for more services? These questions go beyond economic considerations about income distribution. When answering these questions, state legislators consider the political ramifications for their own careers, for their influence within the legislature, and for the development of policies they believe benefit their constituents (Mayhew 1974; Fenno 1978).

Even when taxes or services are held constant, legislators may find that the means of taxation matters for citizens' perceptions about their benefit/tax ratios. If legislators can hide or obscure tax burdens by shifting from obvious "lumpy" property taxes to less hidden, incremental sales and business taxes, they may create the perception of higher benefit/tax ratios when in reality they have only obscured a portion of the tax denominator.

In the remainder of this chapter, I explain three variables that influence the policy process. I present the political avenues federalism creates in U.S. politics. These avenues are the parameters created by the incentives and constraints among levels of government. They go beyond strict economic parameters to include constitutional and statutory arrangements. In the second section, I outline why it is vital to consider the unique nature of public goods. The nonexclusionary nature of public goods has implications for representation and responsiveness even when governments are examined unilaterally. These implications become more complex in federal systems, and federal politics emanate from this complexity. Conversely, legislators' ability to mobilize and take advantage of political resources from particular constituencies and interest groups may encourage them to provide particular benefits programs. An integral part of the importance of public goods revolves around the taxes elected officials choose and whether those taxes connect directly to specific public programs. Tax policy, which is very much connected to governments' responsibility to provide public goods, is the third variable of interest.

The Avenues of Federalism

Changing Incentives in a Federal System

Federalism changes the economic incentives state legislators confront when making policy decisions (Chubb 1985). Federal assistance in the form of matching, categorical, and block grants shifts state budget constraints. In economic parlance, state governments' production-possibilities curves shift when the federal government offers financial assistance. In addition to these objective changes, federalism changes state politics. State legislators operate in a political environment influenced—at times dominated—by federal policies and politics. In this section, I outline how federalism objectively changes the incentives and constraints state legislators face.

The arrangements between U.S. national and state governments and state and local governments shape the avenues on which politicians create federal politics. The revenue and spending arrangements generate tensions among governments and unintended consequences that one or more levels of government must resolve. At times, resolution comes as the result of cooperative accommodations, as in the case of school finance reform in Michigan. At other times, resolutions are more unilateral, as in the case of Tennessee's Medicaid reform, although even in that case federal waivers enabled Tennessee to take action. In some circumstances, actors in both levels of government fail to find solutions to what may appear to be pressing problems. Legislatures and federal or local officials fail to enact policy changes, and problems continue.

Spending in a Federal System

Federal grants take three basic forms. The federal government makes block grants to subnational governments for various categories of services (e.g., transportation and education). In some cases, such as federal revenue sharing in the 1970s, block grants can be completely unrestricted, and states may spend funds in any manner (Brown, Fossett, and Palmer 1984). Federal matching grants provide additional funding for a specific program, the cost of which is borne by both the federal and state governments (Chubb 1985). The Aid to Families with Dependent Children, Medicaid, and interstate highway programs are examples of federal-state programs in which matching rates are computed according to state per capita income. Categorical grants provide funds for a specific state government program or project (Meltsner 1971).

An understanding of the economic effects of federal grants requires discussion of income and substitution effects. Income effects occur when consumers' income rises and they consequently purchase more goods. Similarly, if the price of goods falls, consumers can think of the price drop in the same way they would an income increase. They can now buy more goods than they did before.

Substitution effects occur when the price of Good A falls relative to Good B. In this case, the consumer may consume more of Good A and less of Good B as a result of the relative price changes. Whatever marginal increase in the consumption of A occurs because of the rise in B's price is the substitution effect of the change in the relative prices of the two goods. By offering various forms of grants, the federal government changes the budget constraints and costs of providing benefits. In so doing it creates a new politics for state officials, whose utilization of federal assistance may increase the overall level of benefits they offer but also may change state spending priorities.

Figure 1 depicts a state government and its choices between providing public goods and particular benefits. I begin with the government taxing its citizens to provide an amount of revenue represented by the budget line AB. This revenue could provide either an amount, A, of public goods or a second amount, B, of particular benefits if the government chose to provide only one or the other. A more likely scenario is one in which the government provides some combination of public goods and particular benefits represented in this case by point z on line AB.

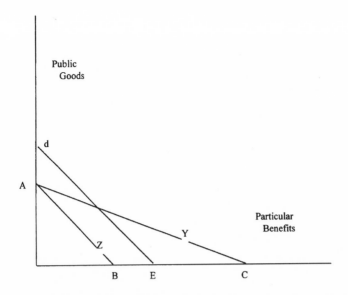

Fig. 1. Trade-offs among public good and particular benefits, and the influence of intergovernmental grants

Assume the federal government accords state governments matching grants for particular benefits: the federal government provides one dollar for every dollar state governments spend. These grants make particular benefits less expensive relative to public goods. If a state wanted to provide only particular benefits, it could now provide twice as many as it did with no grant at a particular level of taxation. Line *AC* represents this budget line change. The line has pivoted around point *A*. In all likelihood, the state will choose to provide more particular benefits and more public goods as a result of the matching grant. This new point of government provision is point *y* on line *AC.*

If the federal government provides an unrestricted block grant, state revenue shifts outward to the right in the figure. At a specific level of taxation, a state can provide more of both public goods and particular benefits, and there has been no change in the relative prices of goods and benefits. In figure 1, this shift moves the original budget line *AB* to the line *DE.* The government may choose to use some of its block grant as a substitute for its own tax revenues, in which case its budget line will also shift between *DE* and line *AB* (Gramlich 1990; Chubb 1985).[2]

Taxes in a Federal System

Governments have the power to extract revenues from their citizens and universally do so. However elected officials cannot engage in limitless taxation because they face electoral as well as economic constraints (Levi 1987; Lowery and Sigelman 1981). In federal systems, elected officials face further constraints but also enjoy new avenues for raising revenues (Key 1956; Riker 1987; Conlan 1988). Federalism introduces two specific issues for state legislators—horizontal rate competition and vertical base competition.

Vertical base competition happens when different levels of governments utilize the same tax bases and find themselves constrained by the decisions of other levels. The federal government relies on income and wage taxes for its revenues, and local governments rely more on property taxes although increasingly they have utilized sales and wage taxes. State governments have relied on the most varied combinations of tax bases—sales, income, property, and various business taxes (Phares 1980). These combinations lead state governments to compete with federal and local governments for limited tax bases. In the case of income taxes, many state legislators noted that although federal rates declined in the 1980s, the increase in social security wage (FICA) taxes and the relatively low threshold for upper brackets on federal income taxes left states with little latitude for increasing state income tax rates.

Vertical base competition becomes salient under two conditions. First whenever one level of government raises a specific tax, it necessarily constrains the remaining tax base. In addition to the structural constraint, the act of raising the tax can increase the political attention voters pay to that tax and make citizens resist further tax increases. This was the case with income taxes following the federal rate increases in 1990 and 1993.

Vertical base competition can also become salient during economic recessions. When revenues contract for all levels of government, officeholders may seek to continue funding services. Because all levels of government may be searching for revenues, they will more likely compete for the same tax bases.

Horizontal rate competition is not as explicit as vertical base competition. It arises from the competition among states to foster healthy tax bases by attracting employers, development, and relatively high-income citizens (Tiebout 1956; Eisinger 1988; Dye 1990). State politicians recognize their neighboring states' tax rates and do not want their own rates too far afield of them. As a result, a downward pressure exerts itself on state tax rates, and within any state this pressure targets taxes that are particularly out of line. For example, in Michigan property taxes were considerably higher both as a percentage of assessed value and particularly as a percentage of family income, but the state's 4 percent retail sales tax was low relative to other Great Lakes states. Consequently, the state traded relatively high property taxes for a reduction on homestead property taxes and an increase, to 6 percent, in the sales tax rate.

The federal nature of government programs and revenue systems creates new politics by complicating legislators' calculations about the costs and benefits of government goods and services. No longer can legislators assume citizens will reelect them based on state taxes and spending. With overlapping finances come overlapping responsibilities, and state representatives must consider state, national, and local taxes and programs when enacting their own policies and budgets.

If each level of government has clearly delineated responsibilities and shares no responsibilities, ascribing responsibility for taxes and for goods and services is straightforward. Policymakers claim credit only for those programs their governments administer and impose taxes directly with no intergovernmental transfers or subsidies. In such a federal system, citizens could assess the goods and services based on the taxes they pay to each level of government. However, in many federal systems, government revenues and spending substantially overlap, and information is neither complete nor symmetric for either citizens or legislators (Riker 1987; Levi 1987). Consequently, policymakers risk blame for unpopular policies or taxes outside their jurisdiction. However, they also can claim credit for popular government programs similarly outside of their realms of responsibility.

The introduction of nonexclusionary goods further complicates governing for elected officials in federal systems. A nonexclusionary good, such as a road or a recreation area, provided by a subnational government may provide benefits to citizens who pay no taxes to that government. In other cases, competition for economic growth and jobs may deter subnational governments from internalizing negative externalities, such as air and water pollution. For example, competition for jobs may lead Ohio officials not to enforce clean air standards. Consequently, New Englanders suffer the effects of acid rain and bear the cost of this negative externality as Ohio's government seeks to protect its job and tax bases.

Public Goods

Although economists have paid considerable attention to public goods, political science inquiry into their provision has largely focused on issues such as "free riders." A different set of questions concerns how federalism affects the provision of public goods by subnational governments. How do competing governments decide which goods to offer, and how much concern is there among officeholders about the efficiency with which and means by which goods are offered?

Do legislators attempt to connect price systems—taxes—to various public goods? Most legislators noted a willingness on the part of constituents to pay for roads and education but a reluctance to pay for public-health programs. Many representatives bemoaned a lack of citizen awareness about the costs of environmental and safety regulations that nonetheless effectively, if indirectly, provide public goods such as clean water and safe workplaces.

If legislators are seen as managers of firms that produce nonexclusionary public goods, then the task they face involves opaque estimates about citizens' demands for public services and how to pay for those services. Buchanan summarizes the dilemma of a state representative well when he writes:

> Decisions on the demand side of public goods are made through political, not market, institutions, and there is no analogue to competitive order that eases the analytic task. (Buchanan 1968, 5)

Whereas firm managers trading private goods can look to price and quantity fluctuations to gauge production, politicians find themselves in a nebulous situation. When they decide to provide a public good, it is available to all citizens. In some cases, citizens may not take advantage of a specific public good, such as a road, but will take advantage of other public goods—other roads—such that they will not notice their lack of utility from a specific good. In other cases, citizens may involuntarily consume public goods—for example, cleaner air or water. Citizens may or may not value these goods directly, but legislators may surmise that citizens should still pay taxes toward them because such public goods also provide positive externalities such as cost savings on future health services that will not be necessary if the clean air results in better physical health.

Federalism creates a new process for deciding what is a public good and how to provide that good. With a unitary government, a single government decides the scope of benefits, financing, populations served, and program administration. Federalism subjects these elements to debate and modification. Even across equivalent governments such as state legislatures, representatives view differently the same policies (e.g., Medicaid and economic development). In the Northwest and Vermont, legislators argued that health care, even in the United States, is a nonexclusionary good because no one is denied care when it is absolutely needed. In Tennessee, representatives believed some elements of health care were nonexclusionary but that others were best handled via private production. In Mississippi, health care was not on the legislature's agenda to any discernable extent.

Public Goods and Particular Benefits

Because public goods are nonexclusionary, consumption by one citizen does not decrease availability of the good for other citizens (Gramlich 1990). Governments and citizens confront supply-and-demand functions unlike those of private firms and consumers, and legislators enjoy an opportunity (largely unique to government) to offer citizens goods from which all may benefit without decreasing benefits for others. Conversely, legislators are confronted with a challenge not faced by private firms—to devise pricing mechanisms (taxes) that reflect citizens' willingness and ability to pay for public goods.

Legislators may decide to tax people such that those who value public goods the most will pay more for them than those citizens who value them less or who do not consume them. By doing so, legislators better match the demand and supply of public goods with citizen preferences for those goods. Consequently, legislators maximize the number of citizens who have a positive consumer surplus.

Considering that governments spend considerable resources on public goods, the question arises of how best to pay for these public goods. The work of Erik Lindahl suggests that in a world with complete information, citizens would reveal their true preferences (i.e., willingness to pay) to the government, which would tax them accordingly. Before moving to an examination of Lindahl taxation, I note that the demand for public goods is determined graphically by vertically summing citizens' willingness to pay for a particular public good. In contrast, demand for private goods is determined by horizontally adding consumers' demand for a product at a given price. For example, if two citizens are willing to pay four hundred and six hundred dollars, respectively, for national defense, then the government could spend one thousand dollars in that arena. This amount of national defense represents the economically efficient point for public supply and demand.

The mechanism for extracting payment is critical to the government's decisions about service levels. For example, if the government decides to offer a referendum on the amount of a good to provide, then the preferences of the median voter will prevail. In figure 2, the government could gain support for a good up to three times the amount of Citizen B's willingness to pay because Citizen B is the median voter and would vote to pay an amount, *P2,* for a public good whether she was paying a head tax or a Lindahl shares tax. Citizen A would have to pay a greater share of the burden for the good than he is willing to pay, Citizen C would pay less than she is willing to pay, and the government would supply quantity *X*. If, however, all citizens revealed their true preferences, then everyone would pay exactly according to their willingness to pay, and the government could supply quantity *Y,* indicated by the intersection of the line denoting the marginal cost of services and the aggregate demand curve. This amount is larger than the amount that would be created if tax shares for all three voters equaled those of the median voter, Citizen B.

Using a referendum process, Citizen A prefers Lindahl taxation to a tax determined by the average cost (cost/3) of providing a public good because he now pays according to his willingness to pay and faces no coercive taxes above that amount. Citizen B is better off because she now pays exactly what she paid under the median voter system, but the government supplies more of the public good. Citizen C loses economic surplus because her taxes increase. However, she is compensated somewhat by the increase in the amount of the public good supplied. Unfortunately, the assumptions that legislators enjoy perfect information and that citizens honestly reveal their preferences are not met in modern state governments. Legislators are left to make their best estimates about service levels and tax systems.

The political argument for imposing a Lindahl tax system to provide public goods addresses the question of how much citizens stand to lose in the absence of various public goods. Higher-income citizens should pay more for certain public goods than should lower-income citizens because they stand to lose more if the good is not provided. Narrowly, national defense and environmental standards afford citizens the same protections

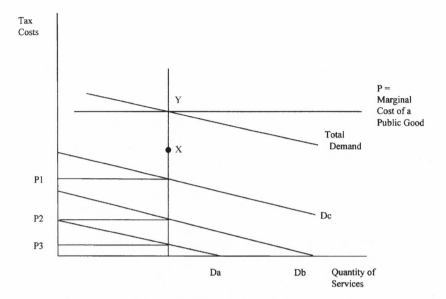

Fig. 2.   Demand and supply of public goods

from foreign threats and various pollutions, yet the costs of not having such protections would be felt more keenly by a higher-income individual. Whereas a poor individual who becomes disabled due to an environmental hazard may lose ten thousand dollars in annual income, a wealthier individual may stand to lose ten or twenty times that amount from the same hazard.

A second political justification for Lindahl taxation involves a consideration of benefit/tax ratios. If legislators wish to maximize the number of constituents whose benefit/tax ratios are equal to or greater than one, then Lindahl taxation provides a mechanism for doing so. Because governments tax citizens according to willingness to pay, citizens who pay Lindahl tax shares receive positive utility from public goods. In other words, every citizen should enjoy a positive difference—a consumer or economic surplus—between the benefits a public good provides and the taxes paid for it.

Legislators provide a mix of public goods and particular benefits. Examples of public goods include national defense, public lands, and a community's income distribution (Jackson and Hawthorne 1987). Examples of particular benefits include AFDC benefits and the home-mortgage-interest deduction. Some government-provided goods have characteristics of both public goods and particular benefits. For example, state-subsidized higher education provides particular benefits for college students, and positive externalities may also exist for the entire community, including having an educated populace, which may help attract employers, or the provision of public land or cultural and athletic performances.

Because public goods benefit all citizens and would be underproduced in private markets, legislators have incentives to give priority to public goods over particular benefits when deciding where to spend limited resources. There are two reasons for this preference. First, legislators cannot target benefits only to their own constituents. The need to assemble majority coalitions behind policy alternatives encourages offering broad-based benefits (Krehbiel 1991). Because public goods offer widely available benefits, legislators should find greater support for offering programs with broad nonexclusionary benefits than for programs with very targeted benefits. Thus, the institutional barriers to building support for a public good are lower than those for particular benefits.

In conjunction with this first reason, public goods provide a means for legislators to raise benefit/tax ratios more than they could with particular benefits. Assume a society has three citizens who each pay ten dollars in taxes. The legislature considers two programs. Program A offers particular benefits to Citizen 1; Program B is a public good offering benefits to all three citizens. Both programs cost thirty dollars. Table 2 illustrates how,

TABLE 2. Public Goods and Particular Benefits

	Tax	Citizen Benefits	Benefit – Tax	Benefit/Tax Ratio
A: A $30 Particular-Benefits Program				
Citizen 1	$10	$38	$28	3.8
Citizen 2	$10	$0	–$10	0
Citizen 3	$10	$0	–$10	0
Totals	$30	$38	$8	
B: A $30 Public Good				
Citizen 1	$10	$8	–$2	0.8
Citizen 2	$10	$15	$5	1.5
Citizen 3	$10	$15	$5	1.5
Totals	$30	$38	$8	

by offering a public good, the legislature can disperse benefits such that all citizens enjoy positive consumer surpluses and will support officeholders. In the first column are taxes. The second column depicts citizens' valuations, or the monetary utility they receive from government programs. The third column shows consumer surpluses, which are the differences between valuations and taxes.

In table 2A, Citizen 1 values the benefits she receives from the government in excess of the costs of producing the good and in excess of her tax burden. Because Citizens 2 and 3 receive no benefits, they have benefit/tax ratios equal to zero, and there is a negative difference between their benefits received and taxes paid. Assuming a majority of citizens elect the government, these citizens would vote for a new government that would stop providing the particular benefits program to Citizen 1 and instead provide the public good depicted in table 2B. The public good creates positive benefit/tax ratios for Citizens 2 and 3 equal to 1.5. Although Citizen 1 has a negative value between her benefits received, eight dollars, and tax paid, ten dollars, she still receives more utility from the public good than Citizens 2 and 3 receive from the particular benefits program.

If the government of this three-citizen community decided it wanted to tax people such that everyone had a benefit/tax ratio greater than one, it could raise taxes by $1.50 on Citizens 2 and 3 and lower them by three dollars for Citizen 1. In this case, every person would enjoy positive differences between benefits and taxes, although Citizens 2 and 3 would see their benefit/tax ratios decline from 1.5 to 1.3.

This preference for public goods does not imply that legislators shy away from providing benefits for specific constituents. Particular benefits, precisely because they are targeted, may provide representatives with the means to mobilize greater political resources (i.e., votes or campaign contributions) than can public goods. Consequently, benefit/tax ratios are one component in representatives' tax-and-spending calculus.

A majority of legislators may benefit politically by promoting a particular benefits program. Assisting a small minority may cost the state little but pay disproportionate political dividends. For example, Mississippi exempts farm equipment from its sales tax ostensibly because it contributes to the production of food. About this policy, a representative explained,

> Well, it doesn't make much sense. We exempt farm equipment from the sales tax because it's used in producing food. So we say farm

equipment is a necessity to the well-being of Mississippians, but then we go and tax food. Now, once upon a time, we didn't tax food, but . . . we changed that and now have this program which helps a farmer buy a hundred thousand dollar combine or cotton picker tax free so he can sell his cotton cheaper to L. L. Bean or somebody, for Christ's sake. It's insane, but the farmers love it and remember us for protecting it every time they buy a hand rake, and nobody really misses the money. So I don't see us changing it.

A second reason why legislators may support particular benefits is that they are politically popular—certain groups may be viewed by the public and legislators as deserving government benefits not accruing to other citizens. Conversely, some groups enjoy little political support, and funding particular benefits programs may falter as a consequence. Legislators spoke frequently of the lack of political support for the Medicaid program, which offered benefits to poor families with an unemployed head but not to the working poor.

Legislators have an implicit model for deciding how to fund particular benefits programs based on whether citizens perceive beneficiaries as deserving and are aware of the benefits and costs of a program. In table 3, legislators can sustain particular benefits programs for deserving beneficiaries even when citizens are aware of the costs of those programs. When citizens are not aware of the costs of benefits for deserving beneficiaries, the programs are highly sustainable. Legislators can also sustain programs for beneficiaries who may not be viewed as deserving if the costs of the program are small or not known to most citizens. Elected officials often cannot sustain programs when citizens resist the costs of a program and perceive its beneficiaries as undeserving.

Federalism intrudes on this basic decision framework for providing public goods and particular benefits. Federalism changes decision parameters by making some programs less expensive relative to others, by

TABLE 3.   Legislators' Particular-Benefits Typology

Benefiting	Costs	
	Known	Unknown
Deserving	Sustainable	Highly Sustainable
Undeserving	Unsustainable	Sustainable

changing the distribution of costs and benefits associated with providing public goods, and by creating competition for tax bases (U.S. Advisory Commission 1993). Amid these constraints and incentives, state legislators sustain their goal of maximizing the benefit/tax ratios for their constituents, but the calculus becomes complicated when multiple layers of government compete and cooperate to provide citizens goods and services.

Having the metric, benefit/tax ratios, for evaluating legislators' policy positions and collective decisions along with the independent factors including federal arrangements, public goods, and taxes, enables consideration of how legislators arrive at collective decisions. For their individual decisions, legislators largely rely on a set of six principles. In developing policy and arriving at collective decisions, several other variables come into play. These variables include the governor's role, overlapping federal and local politics, partisan control of the legislature, current tax system, urgency of changing a particular policy, policy linkages, and resources available for changing one policy without changing either spending for other programs or taxes.

Chapter 3

Representatives' Positions and
Collective Decisions

In this chapter, I connect the parameters of federalism, public goods, and taxes to state representatives' individual issue positions and state legislatures' collective decisions. Representatives rely on a fairly stable set of guiding principles when developing positions about intergovernmental policies. The emphasis given to different principles varies over time, across states, and from issue to issue, but the principles themselves remain stable. In arriving at collective decisions, a variety of economic, institutional, and political factors interact with the principles and positions of individual legislators. These interactions form much of the politics within which state legislatures produce public policy.

Individual Legislators' Positions

Table 4, first presented in chapter 2, depicts changes in taxes and services and the resultant changes in benefit/tax ratios. From this table it can be surmised that elected officials would rather focus their efforts on the options in the upper right-hand section, all of which indicate improved benefit/tax ratios. Representatives prefer to avoid the lower left section, where benefit/tax ratios decrease. Nonetheless, legislators must occasionally consider decreasing benefit/tax ratios—raising taxes and cutting services—or work in the nebulous cells in which both taxes and services either increase or decrease. When legislators do so, they use their governing principles to hold constant or, preferably, improve benefit/tax ratios. When benefit/tax ratios must decrease, representatives justify such decreases or attempt to placate voters by making policies as palatable as possible.

In deciding whether to change services and taxes and, if so, how, state representatives rely on six governing principles. At times, a single principle may dominate all others, or the political symbolism of a specific issue, such as income taxes, may trump legislators' principles. But generally, these six principles—accountability, equity, dependability, obscurability, horizontal transferability, and vertical transferability interact and shape state representatives' positions on policy alternatives.

State legislators may seek to accomplish several goals with any single policy change or combination of policy changes. In addition to calculating changes in their constituents' benefit/tax ratios and estimating a likely distribution of changes for their districts, representatives may seek to garner support from particular groups, such as parents with school-aged children or the elderly, or may attempt to avoid mobilizing opposition from such groups (Denzau and Munger 1986). Legislators may also seek to advance their careers within the legislature or within state politics.

State representatives try to change policies to increase the benefit/tax ratios for most, if not all, of their constituents. Consequently, the principles they emphasize will work to move them to the cells in table 4 that offer unequivocal increases in benefit/tax ratios. When policy changes indicate either increases or decreases in both tax and services, legislators are less certain about changes in benefit/tax ratios, although they may structure policy changes in an effort to increase the probability of an increase for most of their constituents, as chapters 4, 6, and 7 will show. Conversely, representatives may structure changes so that benefit/tax ratio decreases fall on as few citizens as possible.

Governing Principles

In addition to the paradoxical objectives of providing services and not imposing taxes, state representatives may have numerous other personal

TABLE 4. Changes in Government Services, Taxes, and Benefit/Tax Ratio Changes

Services	Taxes		
	Increase	No Change	Decrease
Increase	?	Increase	Increase
No Change	Decrease	No Change	Increase
Decrease	Decrease	Decrease	?

and collective goals. Individually, legislators may seek to increase their influence within state government, to develop good public policies, and to further their own political careers (Fenno 1973). Collectively, state representatives develop policies that allow for stable revenues and expenditures, endeavor to build majority coalitions, and encourage economic development. Regardless of which goals have priority, state representatives find themselves in an ongoing political process, and this chapter outlines the six principles. These principles guide legislators' views and decisions about policies. In addition to the six governing principles, I also discuss the role of political symbolism, direct democracy, and policy history in federal politics.

1. Dependability

Many scholars have noted that state taxes are typically regressive relative to federal taxes. One rationale for regressivity offered by state representatives is that regressive revenues are dependable and provide funds in both good times and bad. Fifty-two percent of the legislators mentioned dependability in the interviews. This figure approached 75 percent in the three states that had no personal income tax.

Revenue dependability becomes a salient principle when representatives seek funding for popular programs. For example, one of the concerns voiced about shifts away from property taxes for public-school funding was that the loss of dependability would leave a very popular public good vulnerable to economic fluctuations. Dependability also becomes germane in states that rely on relatively few taxes. If these states rely on a single cyclical tax for a large proportion of their revenues, then they may seek a second dependable tax to provide revenue stability over time. In Washington, which has no income tax, representatives cited the state's payroll-based business and occupation tax as the stabilizing component in their revenue mix.

Legislators in Washington, Michigan, New Jersey, and New York discussed revenue dependability as a reason for retaining various gross-receipts and utilities taxes. Property tax limitations in Michigan and Massachusetts led representatives either to seek more stable taxes in the form of a graduated income tax (Massachusetts) or to suggest the state is unlikely to move away from its relatively stable single business tax (Michigan). In Florida and Tennessee, where the governments rely heavily on cyclical consumption taxes, and in Mississippi, where gambling revenues have recently made state coffers flush, representatives spoke of the need to find more stable revenue bases such as income taxes or to establish spending practices that would safeguard against revenue fluctuations.[1]

Representatives may seek dependability as a means of decreasing the probability of having to decrease citizens' benefit/tax ratios. Although dependability may come at the expense of other principles, such as equity or vertical transferability, it enables legislators to provide stable bundles of goods and services. The advantage of dependability is that it helps legislators avoid having to decrease services with every economic fluctuation in a state's economy. Although citizens might benefit marginally with more progressive or obvious taxes in an objective economic sense, they also might react negatively to having services slashed or tax rates hiked frequently.

In some respects, legislators' perceptions about revenue dependability are at odds with the economics of taxation. Although sales taxes fluctuate less than income taxes during economic recessions, most legislators in states relying exclusively on sales taxes said that their revenues fluctuated more than they would have with an income tax. From one perspective, this is a valid perception. If these states adopted income taxes in addition to their sales taxes, they would enjoy greater revenue stability (Gold 1988). However, if they adopted income taxes to replace the sales taxes, their revenues would fluctuate more during recessions. Another factor complicating dependability is the sales tax base itself (Galper and Pollock 1988). States that tax necessities, such as food, utilities, and clothing, suffer less cyclical fluctuation than their counterparts that exempt such items from their sales tax base. Although income taxes are more responsive to short-term economic fluctuations than are sales taxes, states that rely more heavily on income taxes have enjoyed greater long-term revenue growth as personal incomes have risen (Phares 1980; Galper and Pollock 1988). Because most states have not taxed services and retained only merchandise sales tax bases, state governments have experienced a lack of responsiveness in the overall revenue growth as the service sector of the economy has grown relative to retail trade (Galper and Pollock 1988; Francis 1988).

2.   Horizontal Transferability

A favored means for minimizing tax burdens results from shifting taxes onto citizens from other jurisdictions. Many legislators support taxes that are borne by people from outside the state (Phares 1980). In Florida and

Nevada, large tourism industries export a significant portion of tax burdens to nonresidents. Forty-four percent of legislators discussed horizontal transferability as an influence on state policy. Legislators in Colorado, Florida, and Vermont, which have large tourism industries, referred to horizontal transferability more frequently than their counterparts in other states.

The importance of horizontal transferability depends on a state's demographics and economics. States with large tourism industries have the ability to "export" much of their tax needs, yet representatives in these states voiced concerns that doing so left their citizens with unrealistic expectations about the true costs and benefits of government. The other way in which horizontal transferability becomes engaged is when representatives perceive that nonresidents have the opportunity to benefit from their states' public goods without paying the taxes to provide those goods. In these cases, representatives seek to find means to end out-of-state free riding on their states' nonexclusionary programs.

In many respects, horizontal transferability is an extension of the benefits-received principle. Tourists enjoy the benefits of state-provided public goods, such as roads and recreational facilities. In turn, state policymakers are only too happy to see such nonresidents pay sales taxes. But horizontal transferability goes beyond the benefits-received principle in that legislators seek tourist revenues that exceed the costs of providing public goods to visitors. Such "excess" revenues can then be used to lower taxes for residents and increase the difference between the utility residents receive from government and the taxes they pay for it. Horizontal transferability is a response to the dilemma subnational governments face when providing public goods. For nonresidents, a second state's nonexclusionary goods represent a clear windfall unless this second state can impose a tax on visitors to collect a contribution for the public goods they enjoy. For example, when Michigan slashed its property taxes, it did so only on homestead property, leaving vacation property—much of it along Lake Michigan owned by Chicagoans—taxed at relatively high rates.

I offer two additions to the traditional public-finance definitions of exportability or horizontal transferability. First, tax reciprocity, or what might be called tax drain, occurs when the tax policies of a particular state, in conjunction with neighboring states' policies, lead citizens to avoid paying state taxes by transacting their business in neighboring states. Consequently, the first state loses revenue because of a tax policy. Tax drain was an issue in Tennessee, where there is a broad-based 8 percent sales tax and no personal income tax. Some legislators supported high sales tax rates because tourists then paid more to the state treasury than they would have at lower rates. Other House members countered that many Tennesseans go to other states to avoid Tennessee's sales tax. Consequently, "fiscal drain" losses outweighed any advantages from exportability. Estimates by the Tennessee House Ways, Means, and Finance Committee indicate that the state loses $300 million annually in revenue because people buy groceries in neighboring states to avoid Tennessee's 8 percent tax on food.

Compounding the fiscal-drain problem is Tennessee's lack of an income tax. As a consequence of not having an income tax, Tennessee has no tax reciprocity with its neighbors for those citizens who work in one state but reside in another. People who work in Kentucky and live in Tennessee pay only Kentucky income taxes. People who live in Kentucky and work in Tennessee also pay only Kentucky income taxes. If Tennessee had an income tax, its legislature would likely arrange reciprocity agreements with neighboring states for such individuals. Such agreements are common among states.[2]

Reciprocity and fiscal-drain revenue losses can be substantial. Several legislators and staffers estimated that Tennessee loses $150–300 million every year from this lack of reciprocity, as much as 4 percent of Tennessee's annual general fund.

The second problem states avoid is becoming a service importer. Although states seek to export tax burdens, legislators do not wish to provide services to persons beyond their borders. Colorado and Washington representatives complained that Californians increasingly sought admission to their public universities. University administrators found these students attractive because of their academic profiles and their obligation to pay revenue-yielding out-of-state tuition. However, more nonresidents also means fewer in-state students, which results in disgruntled constituents who have no enthusiasm for subsidizing Californians' higher educations.

3. Vertical Transferability

I make a distinction between transferring tax burdens across jurisdictions and transferring tax burdens from one level of government to another (see Phares 1980; Dye 1990). The former connotes horizontal transferability, and the latter is vertical transferability. In most cases, legislators view vertical transferability as federal or local governments paying a greater share of goods and services. However, in some instances legislators felt they better served their constituents when the state assumed financial responsibility for certain program costs. Legislators in Michigan, Mississippi, New Jersey, Vermont, and Washington explicitly argued that the state could better access revenues and more equitably distribute funds for education than could localities. In Massachusetts, continuing fiscal difficulties in the wake of Proposition 2½ led many legislators to call for greater assistance to localities for education. In New York, assembly members similarly argued in favor of the state's assumption of Medicaid costs. Overall, 48 percent of the legislators mentioned vertical transferability in terms of having the federal and local governments assume a greater proportion of government expenditures. Thirty-six percent of legislators discussed vertical transferability and said that the ability of the state to access and distribute tax dollars equitably justified state assumption of program costs from localities.

Vertical transferability becomes salient when intergovernmental programs enter a crisis and during economic recessions. With regard to recessions, officeholders will naturally look to other levels of government to maintain services when their own revenues contract. Doing so enables officeholders to maintain their constituents' benefit/tax ratios. Perhaps more interesting, vertical transferability becomes a feature in policymaking when programs have lost or begin to lose political support. If legislators perceive a lack of support for a specific program, they may seek to lessen their government's responsibility for that program. Less politically, if the costs of a program rise dramatically and unexpectedly, legislators may seek additional assistance from the federal government because their government lacks the resources or would have to dramatically shift resources to continue funding a program. If the steeply increasing costs erode political support for the program, then legislators may find themselves in a spiral whereby they may shift costs from popular programs, decreasing the benefit/tax ratios for citizens who use those programs, to fund an unpopular program whose increasing costs contribute to its unpopularity.

When tax systems interact, policymakers recognize the tax-base competition that transpires among levels of government and the need for governments to accommodate one another lest one or both levels face negative political or electoral consequences. For example, the federal income tax allows for deductibility of state income taxes. This deductibility means state tax rates are offset by a reduction in the federal government's income tax base. More implicitly, several states offer circuit breakers (state income tax relief) to offset citizens' local property tax liabilities. Initially, such relief does not appear to be a recognition of tax-base competition, because states tax income and localities tax property. However, legislators noted that the vast majority of people pay local property taxes with income generated from their labor rather than with income generated from property. Consequently, circuit breakers in states like Vermont and Michigan compensate for local taxes on current income.

Although one might expect state legislators to promote lower state taxes, the local basis of their election—cities, towns, and counties—and the states' dominant position over localities lead many state representatives to recognize the tax interdependence between state and local governments. This recognition induces a willingness, sometimes even enthusiasm, among state legislators to raise taxes as a means of lowering local property tax burdens and ameliorating resource differences among local communities.

In addition to revenue interactions, many representatives discussed "drawing down" federal dollars to increase the amount of state-provided goods and services. In so doing, legislators act as if federal taxes are fixed and then work to maximize their citizens' total tax/benefit ratios (i.e., the tax/benefit ratio for all federal, state, and local taxes) by designing programs that will maximize the amount of federal funding flowing to the state. Even very conservative legislators who espoused views favoring very limited government supported bringing federal dollars to their states as a means of increasing the return on the tax dollar for their constituents.

4. Obscurability

Obscurability, or fiscal illusion, refers to the ability of policymakers to impose taxes that go unnoticed by taxpayers (Phares 1980; Hansen 1983; Dye 1990; Steuerle 1991). Because obscuring taxes creates a perception of greater benefit/tax ratios, representatives can almost always be expected to attempt to obscure some taxes. However, in connection to spending, representatives may seek obscure taxes to fund particular benefit programs. If legislators can mobilize substantial political resources by providing particular benefits and imposing no costs on the beneficiaries, then it is unsurprising that they do so. But providing particular benefits may also mobilize resentment among voters who do not benefit. Consequently, obscure revenues provide the means by which to fund particular benefits without mobilizing voter opposition. Creative legislators may find ways to combine revenue transfers, either horizontal or vertical, with obscure revenues to provide a sizable array of particular benefits.

In its most narrow sense, fiscal illusion implies that taxpayers are completely unaware of taxes. Examples include excise or corporate income taxes that firms pass on to consumers and embed in final prices. In other instances, citizens may be aware of the tax but unaware of their total tax burdens. These taxes would include sales taxes, which citizens generally pay in small increments (Steuerle 1991; Dye 1990).

I use the broader definition of fiscal illusion. Fiscal illusion takes place when constituents cannot accurately assess the burden from a specific tax. Thirty-two percent of legislators mentioned obscurability as a determinant of tax policy. Many suggested that state sales taxes are regarded as the least politically harmful tax to raise because citizens do not know their sales tax liabilities and would have difficulty tracking them. Whereas citizens can see payroll deductions for state and federal income and wage taxes, they find the task of tracking sales taxes daunting. As one Tennessee legislator explained in discussing why his constituents would oppose an income tax even if such a change implied eliminating the sales tax, "We in Tennessee have been trained to pay our taxes fifty cents a day in increments of about a nickel. Now even if you came out and gave them a dollar a week tax, they'd hate it because they'd recognize it as a tax and not an orange or a candy bar."

In one sense, obscuring taxes can be viewed as policymakers' responses to an unwillingness on the part of citizens to report accurately the utility they receive from government goods and services (Samuelson 1954). The ability of legislators to hide taxes offers an avenue by which governments can compensate for Samuelson's contention that citizens underreport their willingness to pay for public goods. If citizens are unaware of their tax burdens, then legislators have at least one mechanism by which to finance levels of goods and services that genuinely comport with citizens' preferences rather than just with citizens' reported, or underreported, willingness to pay.

Fiscal illusion influences which taxes representatives cut. Cutting unnoticed or obscure taxes pays few, if any, political dividends, whereas cutting more noticeable income and property taxes creates an opportunity for larger political benefits and an appreciative constituency. Representatives concentrate on reducing highly publicized corporate profit taxes and individual income tax rates instead of other taxes such as gross receipts and utility taxes even when these taxes are more onerous to businesses and individuals. Taxes with low visibility are simply less politically advantageous to decrease. Additionally, legislators suggest that these taxes are not cut because they offer dependable revenue streams and because there would be little political dividend in reducing them.

To some extent, the obscurability of a specific tax is determined by how the tax is collected. Scholars agree that consumers ultimately pay various gross-receipts business taxes, yet they never see these taxes because merchants incorporate them into prices. In other cases, obscurability is a function of the divisibility of the tax. Citizens may know they pay retail sales taxes, but tracking sales tax burdens is difficult because they pay it in varied increments. One might perceive obscurability as a continuum, with embedded excise taxes being the most obscure, followed by sales taxes and more obvious income and property taxes.

5. Accountability

Accountability can be conceptualized in terms of policy accountability and political accountability. Policy accountability implies that constituents are willing to pay a specific tax for a specific purpose and are aware of both. Political accountability occurs when voters support or reject changes in broad-based taxes predicated on their perceptions of how well governments deliver goods and services. Policy accountability is an important feature of popular public-goods programs provided via broad-based taxes. Because all citizens can consume the public good, representatives will seek to establish the policy accountability such that citizens will perceive the good as necessary, efficiently produced, and as a program from which all citizens should benefit.

With political accountability, representatives' focus shifts to finding palatable taxes to finance public goods that enjoy policy accountability. Political accountability—citizen support for government writ large—becomes a concern when governments undertake major reforms or face a crisis with a specific program. With education, representatives perceived that local property taxes had become unacceptable to many constituents and thus threatened the policy accountability of education and the political accountability of state and local governments. Consequently, state representatives acted to decrease objections to local property taxes to sustain support for education and broaden support for their own general government. With health care, representatives sought to contain costs to prevent a further shifting of resources away from more popular programs and to find ways to restore the policy accountability of Medicaid to sustain their governments' political accountability.

I examine policy accountability in discussing taxes on hospital services in Tennessee and sales tax changes in Colorado and Mississippi. The defeat, by referendum, of an extension on the Colorado tourism and cultural taxes and the shift from property to sales taxes in Michigan serve as illustrations of the broader concept of political accountability. Sixty-eight percent of legislators indicated that accountability had significantly shaped recent policy changes in their states.

State representatives' concerns about public goods regarded both policy and political accountability. Representatives frequently lamented the obscurability of certain public goods such as clean air and water and argued that citizens took such goods for granted, were unaware that their taxes provided them, or were unaware of the private health and aesthetic costs to citizens of not providing these public goods.

Federalism clouds both political and policy accountability. In terms of political accountability, many legislators complained that the American federal system has become "government by blob," with little distinction among levels of government and a concomitant distaste for government in general. Because citizens do not distinguish which level of government provides which services, legislators find it difficult to convince citizens to accept specific taxes even when revenues are earmarked for specific purposes. Legislators relayed stories of constituents suggesting that any new, even necessary, services could be providing by trimming waste from state spending.

6. Equity

Although the principle of equity acquires various economic and political connotations, I focus on two definitions of equity as a principle of providing and paying for state services. Some representatives view equity as a matter of an ability to pay, while others view it in terms of deserving to pay (Jewell 1982; Dye 1990; Peterson 1981). In the case of the former, legislators call for progressive taxation and generally oppose particular tax benefits (e.g., employer tax abatements). In the case of the latter, legislators connected the "deserves to pay" concept with government accountability and suggested that user fees not only implemented the deserves-to-pay principle but also enhanced government accountability. Among the representatives interviewed, 88 percent discussed equity, with approximately two-thirds emphasizing the ability-to-pay concept vis-à-vis tax policy and one-third emphasizing the deserves-to-pay principle.

Legislators engaged the ability-to-pay principle for financing public goods but differed in how they defined ability to pay. For some representatives, ability to pay related only to income, whereas others saw it as a function of consumption. The former argued that citizens should pay income taxes and that the state lacked the means to force high-income citizens to spend their money within the state to generate sales tax revenues. The latter group argued that citizens who consumed were demonstrating their ability to pay and that taxes should be attached accordingly.

As I discussed in the previous chapter, a system of Lindahl taxation, which taxes citizens according to their willingness and ability to pay, provides an effective means to achieve equity when equity is defined as ability to pay (Gramlich 1990). Because such a tax system enables governments to tax according to citizen preferences and willingness to pay, it provides a more economically optimal supply of public goods than do tax systems based on per capita costs (Tiebout 1956) or the preferences of the median voter (Gramlich 1990). The requirement that citizens honestly reveal their willingness to pay severely limits the potential to implement such a system. Nonetheless, legislators may consider that because of income effects and decreasing budget constraints, higher-income citizens should pay more for government goods and services than should lower-income citizens. Although legislators may not have perfect information about citizens' preferences, the equity principle leads representatives to favor some form of progressive taxation for the provision of public goods.

User fees and dedicated taxes provide equitable taxation if policymakers emphasize the benefits-received principle. In such cases, the recipients of state services pay for those services via user fees. In some instances, fees can be mixed with more general revenues to internalize externalities inherent in some public goods. For example, a recreational area may require no fee for those who hike or canoe, but a fee might be imposed on those who use recreational vehicles and boats and thus create noise, air, and water pollution (Gramlich 1990).

Representatives recognized that they are sometimes criticized by academics and policymakers for implementing regressive tax systems, but the legislators responded that sales taxes represent the ability-to-pay equity principle if the state exempts necessities such as food from the sales tax base. These legislators reasoned that when citizens improve their well-being by purchasing products, they demonstrate that they have disposable income, a portion of which the state taxes.

Beyond these principles, representatives operate in a context that is shaped by political symbolism, state policy histories, party politics, and the institutional powers enjoyed by legislatures and constituents.

Political Symbolism

Although not a governing principle, political symbols influence federal politics in ways that cannot be captured with simple measurements of expenditures and revenues (Edelman 1964). Legislators in states without income taxes viewed citizen resistance to state personal income taxes as a consequence of federal income and wage taxes. These representatives discussed the income tax as a symbol of unresponsive, inefficient government. They based their opposition to the income tax on this symbolism even when they personally preferred lowering sales taxes and imposing an income tax as a means of lowering state tax burdens on low- and middle-income individuals and families. Forty percent of legislators discussed political symbolism, and more than half of this proportion suggested it influenced their opposition to state income taxes.

Capturing the effects of political symbolism on policy outcomes is more subtle than measuring the effects of other variables common in models of state politics. Yet legislators' reports about the federal government, particularly the politics of income taxes, and the effects of these politics on their views about tax changes were consistent across states. As one Mississippi representative mentioned, "When it came to our sales tax increase, an income tax would have been more fair in many respects . . . but we couldn't touch it because people hate their federal income tax."[3]

I separate symbolism from the governing principles because its role in the federal system is often beyond the control of state legislators. Whereas representatives make decisions to balance their needs for revenue dependability with their desires to obscure revenues, political symbols fall beyond this sphere of decision making. Although legislators may create or sustain certain symbols, citizens' reactions to political symbols determine their influence on legislators (Edelman 1964).

At times, symbolic politics override the incentives and constraints federalism introduces into intergovernmental relations. Despite structural incentives to rely on state income and property taxes, state elected officials may find citizen opposition to such taxes so strong that the officeholders instead shift to sales taxes. State politicians ignore federal incentives and respond to the politics dominating the situation. In other situations, legislators' desires for revenue dependability or for taxes that can be transferred to other jurisdictions may lead them to ignore or reject various federal incentives.

These six principles guide individual legislators in providing and financing state public goods, federal-state, and state-local programs. The principles filter legislators' policy alternatives and contribute to establishing the parameters of policies likely to be enacted. In some cases, one principle, such as obscurability, may trump a combination of other principles, such as accountability, equity, and dependability. Nonetheless, the principles help representatives define the financing mechanisms for any particular policy. Examples of considerations and parameters include whether the tax connects to the service in voters' perceptions as well as in state budget arrangements. Does a tax present an equity concern with respect to whether citizens can afford to pay or deserve to pay? Is an obscure tax available and politically desirable? How necessary is it to find new revenues for a policy change? How necessary is the policy change itself? Can the state expect to grow its way out of a problem with the current tax structure? How will the revenue source react with neighboring states' policies or with federal and local policies?

Of course, a legislator's position on any one issue does not imply that position will become state policy. The political process limits viable policy alternatives, and policies become linked in novel or unexpected ways, forcing legislators to make unexpected compromises. Consequently, a simple examination of how federalism and public goods affect legislators' thinking provides an incomplete picture of representatives' responsiveness in federal politics. To complete the picture, it is necessary to examine how legislators' perceptions of federalism, public goods, and taxes interact with other features of the policy process such that representatives' individual preferences are translated into collective policy decisions.

Collective Decisions

In the following chapters, I analyze a variety of collective decisions and nondecisions by state legislatures. Federalism and individual views about public goods and taxation influenced all of these decisions, whether they concerned tax policy, economic development, education, or health care. In addition, several other political, economic, and contextual variables became relevant. The political variables include party strength and the governor's ideology, party, and policy agendas. Also, the differences across legislative districts and legislators' ability to find common ground that would benefit a broad array of citizens were factors in several cases. The institutional policymaking role of the legislature itself and its ability to define a policy process for a specific problem influenced major decisions in several states. The economic and policy variables that most often played a role in the policy process related to a state's revenue growth and the demands on spending for programs such as Medicaid or education.

The principles that guide legislators' individual views on policies are present again in their collective decisions. Although legislators do not collectively state that one principle or another has guided a specific piece of legislation, I find that because representatives rely on the governing principles there is often widespread agreement on why one policy was preferred to another or why one policy was more politically feasible than a second. At times, legislators may find that despite their own preferences for an ideal policy, one or two of the principles becomes so dominant that they trump all others. For example, the recent political symbolism of cutting income taxes became so dominant in the early 1990s that most legislators indicated that any concerns they had about taxing according to the ability-to-pay principle had to be put aside. In turn, legislators emphasized the principle of tax obscurability, or the deserves-to-pay principle, when revenue increases were absolutely necessary.

Representatives look to their constituencies as both a source of information and a determinant of their support for various policy alternatives (Fenno 1978; Kingdon 1989). Yet the relationship between representatives and their constituents runs both ways. Because policy alternatives may originate in a state capital or even in another state, state legislators spoke of "selling the program" to their constituents, with some policies easier to promote than others. Representatives in ten of eleven case-study states indicated that citizens supported education spending. In Mississippi, Florida, Tennessee, and Michigan legislators sold tax increases with provisos that dedicated marginal revenues to education programs. Conversely, Medicaid expansions were more difficult to sell, and hardest of all for legislators in Washington, Florida, and Tennessee was the prospect of selling a state income tax.

Erikson, Wright, and McIver (1989, 1993) demonstrate that party strength influences the policy outputs in state governments. My findings comport with theirs, and the case studies show how views about public goods and which principles legislators emphasize in their policy choices often break along party lines. The examples also illustrate how divided government, the party and policy agenda of the governor, and the unity of parties within the legislatures influence both which policy alternatives are viable and which alternatives the legislature collectively decides to enact.

Federal or state-local programs and the parameters of individual policies may shape policy reforms or efforts to change the financing of the programs. Any need for federal waivers from policy requirements will likely shape policy proposals at the state level. Just as fundamentally, a state's fiscal condition may affect whether a state decides to take action on a given program and whether that action is intended to reform a program or merely to address an immediate crisis (Kingdon 1990). In the case of the former, Michigan representatives used the latitude in their state's relatively low sales tax to promote a massive $6 billion shift in school funding from localities to the state government. In the case of the latter, representatives in several states, especially Tennessee, noted that during the late 1980s and early 1990s their legislatures had enacted a number of stopgap spending or revenue measures designed to address continually increasing demands on the Medicaid program. Conversely, in Colorado, legislators backed away from a gubernatorial health-reform proposal after the estimated costs of the Medicaid program dropped by an unexpected $200 million in 1994.

Beyond issues of fiscal condition and the budgetary impact of any one program, a state's overall economic profile may influence the undertaking of major policy initiatives and their content (Dye 1990). Even in a state where resources are scarce, such as Mississippi, in 1992 the state legislature enacted a sales tax increase over the objections of the governor as a means of offering more educational services. As I will discuss in chapter 6, the decision to raise the sales tax was based on the political opposition to the income tax and the low property values of many school districts that most needed revenue. In addition, the legislature promoted the sales tax because of political, partisan considerations and because of the distribution of economic resources within the state.

Of course, predicting when states will enact major policy changes, when they will address immediate crises with temporary measures, and when they will fail to decide on policy reforms is neither neat nor fail-safe.

But it is possible to speak in probabilistic terms about changes that are more or less likely and what is expected given a set of political, institutional, and economic variables. In addition to predicting policy changes, it is possible to better understand why states change policies when they do and what role individual political actors play in shaping those policies. State political elites are not mere robots responding to a state's economic climate or agents of their constituents but are complex actors that both influence their state's policies and respond to the policies of other governments.

Each of the following chapters offers something different for the understanding of federalism, public goods, and taxes in state politics. In chapter 4, "Read Our Lips: No New (Income) Taxes," I examine how the political symbolism of the federal income tax has affected state tax politics.

In chapter 5, "Tax and Spend or Spending Taxes—Economic Development in the States," I analyze state economic development. Many representatives view economic growth as a means by which they can continually increase their constituents' benefit/tax ratios. More concretely, economic-development policies offer perhaps the most concrete policy area in which to see the differences among legislators' views about public goods and particular benefits. Some legislators emphasize public goods such as schools and roads as the most effective development tools, while others insist that tax abatements for firms are a more efficient means by which to foster economic growth.

In chapter 6, "Education Financing: How Many Types of Equity?" I present the state and local dilemma that state legislators face as they struggle to provide what many of their state constitutions mandate be treated as a public, nonexclusionary, good—an equal education for every child. As property taxes have climbed and become more disparate across communities and less reflective of citizens' abilities to pay, state representatives have had to contend with both hostile public responses to locally based taxes and, in several states, with court orders mandating the equalization of education funding across school districts.

Chapter 7 shifts from state and local relations to federal-state relations with an analysis of state responses to health-care reform in 1993 and 1994. Most legislators viewed health care as neither a purely public nor purely private good, and concomitantly they differed greatly about how to finance health care. Several thought the current system both inequitable in excluding working poor persons from Medicaid and inefficient in that beneficiaries sought care in expensive emergency rooms and not at general practitioners' offices. Yet the inability of the states to find revenue sources to make Medicaid less exclusive, coupled with uncertainty over federal health-care politics, stalled several states' efforts to revamp their Medicaid programs.

The most fundamental political issues are examined in the next chapter. Without revenues, governments could do little, and the entire issue of public goods versus particular benefits would wither.

Chapter 4

Read Our Lips, No New (Income) Taxes

The federal Tax Reform Act of 1986 offered state governments an incentive to utilize personal income taxes and to decrease their reliance on sales taxes. By maintaining a deduction for state and local income and property taxes and eliminating the deduction for sales taxes, Congress sustained a subsidy of a particular subnational tax while eliminating another. Since 1986, however, only Connecticut has adopted a personal income tax, and the trend among state governments has been away from income taxes toward sales taxes (Gold 1990). State legislators' have several perceptions about why state governments have not responded to the federal incentive for income taxation. Although the 1986 Tax Reform Act encouraged states to adopt income taxes, other federal policies, such as wage tax increases, and the persistent federal politics decrying income taxes created a political climate in which state representatives found it difficult to even propose increases in income tax rates (Steuerle 1991).

In states with and without an income tax, representatives' aversion to income tax increases illustrates how the political costs of a specific policy change can override the objective economic and distributional benefits of the same change. In every state, representatives explained that although they supported progressive income tax increases as a matter of principle and as a matter of economic equity among their constituents, the political firestorms that could result from such tax increases and their subsequent political costs simply made them too risky. With tax policy, legislators perceived that the political costs of taxing according to ability-to-pay principles were likely too high. Consequently, legislators proposed and enacted more obscure tax increases in sales and "hidden" business taxes in the wake of the federal income tax increases in 1990 and 1993.

Legislators' arguments against income taxes focused on citizen dis-

46

dain for federal income and wage taxes and suppositions that state legislators would continually increase income tax rates. Most representatives perceived that constituents resisted sales taxes less than income taxes because of the obscurability of the former. Other arguments favoring sales taxes identified their universal incidence and horizontal transferability. In the case of obscurability, legislators framed their arguments in terms of not overtaxing working individuals via income taxes. With respect to horizontal transfers, legislators argued that sales taxes paid by nonresidents alleviated tax burdens for residents.

Legislators perceive that their constituents loathe income taxes and believe support for income taxes indicates support for "big government." Many suggested that their constituents felt taxes were as high or higher than at the start of the 1980s despite decreases in federal income tax rates in the early 1980s, substantial reform in 1986, and two presidential campaigns in which the winning candidate ran strongly opposed to new or additional taxes.

Income taxes have thus become a political target for citizens who are disgruntled with government and seek a political outlet for their frustrations. With New Jersey's enactment of a substantial income tax increase and the federal enactment of an income tax increase in 1990, income taxes became the "powerful condensation symbol" for various complaints against government (Edelman 1964, 172). Politicians have responded by attempting to reduce income taxes and by not increasing income tax rates even when their states' fiscal conditions are dire. The conflict for state legislators requires balancing funding needs with a political desire to lower income taxes. Consequently, state legislators have declined to utilize an avenue of federalism available to them by choosing sales and excise taxes that cannot be deducted from federal income taxes.

Representatives' perceptions about citizen distrust of taxation find support in public opinion data. A 1993 Gallup Poll reported that 50 percent of citizens thought federal income taxes would be raised unfairly, while 42 percent felt taxes would be increased fairly. Sixty percent of the respondents did not believe that the money raised from a federal income tax increase would be used to reduce the deficit despite pledges by President Bill Clinton and members of Congress to do so (Gallup 1994, 235). Paradoxically, 75 percent of the respondents supported increasing taxes on incomes greater than seventy-five thousand dollars yet demonstrated little support for any tax increases or faith that such increases would be used for their intended purposes. The resistance to income taxes is thus rooted in the distrust that politicians will direct tax increases at those with modest incomes.

A variety of means could provide tax relief that would offer greater tax equity, offer greater revenue dependability, or negatively affect vertical transferability less than would income tax reductions. Yet popular political demands to reduce income taxes override these considerations, and politicians find themselves developing policies in which accommodating an income tax decrease is primary and in which other components depend on the size and nature of the income tax reductions. Many state legislators argued that a lack of latitude to raise income taxes has left their state coffers relatively empty even in flush economic times (see Galper and Pollock 1988). In these circumstances, legislators find themselves unable to provide for programs even when majorities of their colleagues support them.

With income tax politics, legislators referred to all six governing principles. Despite their desire to tax citizens according to the ability-to-pay principle or to vertically transfer taxes onto the federal government by raising federally deductible state income taxes, legislators found that the principle of obscurability and the political symbolism of the income tax preempted their efforts to apply these other principles. In the case of income tax politics, representatives' desires for obscurability trumped other governing principles. In other circumstances, when federal income tax politics are not as salient, other principles may emerge and interact with obscurability, but in the early and mid-1990s, such was rarely the case.

Background

The trend away from income taxes follows a flurry of state tax changes in the 1980s. Concomitant with income tax reductions, states increased sales tax rates. In the early 1980s, states enacted thirty-seven sales tax increases to grapple with fiscal crises created by the severe recession in 1982 and reductions in federal assistance (Gold 1986). Many of these states also raised income tax rates but then lowered them during the late 1980s. While fifteen states lowered income tax rates from 1985 through 1989, only one state lowered its sales tax. Overall, thirty-two states ended the 1980s with higher sales tax rates than they had at the beginning of the decade.[1]

Measured in terms of real dollars and as a percentage of personal income, state tax revenues grew dramatically during the 1960s and 1970s. Indeed, by the 1970s, many states cut income tax rates in response to the revenue bounces as a result of the effects of inflation and increases in tax rates enacted in the previous two decades. The 1980s, however, were a different story. During 1982 and 1983 most states raised sales and income tax rates. Unlike the 1960s, they raised rates at a time when they simultaneously cut spending. States began the 1980s facing reduced federal assistance and the worst economic contraction since the Great Depression (Gold 1982).

By the mid-1980s the economy had recovered enough for most states to have sufficient latitude in their budgets to make tax reductions. Unlike previous periods of enacting new taxes and increasing tax rates, this period of tax change marked a definite shift from progressive taxes to regressive and obscure taxes. Table 5 details the changes in state sales and income tax burdens over time as a proportion of citizens' personal income.[2]

Table 5 depicts income taxes rising to near parity with sales taxes by the late 1980s. Income taxes accounted for 39 percent of state revenues in 1990 but declined to 37 percent by 1993. While this trend is not dramatic, it marks a shift away from income taxes. Many states that increased income tax rates during the 1990–91 recession are now considering large tax reductions.[3] In New Jersey, Governor Christine Todd Whitman has proposed a 30 percent reduction in income tax rates that would more than offset the 1990 increase. In Connecticut and Arizona, successful Republican candidates for governor ran on promises (as yet unfulfilled) to abolish state income taxes.

In addition to the political attention paid to income taxes, the actions of state legislatures further demonstrate shifts from income to sales taxes. In the 1990s, a recession and tight federal fiscal policies led states to increase taxes. During 1991 and 1992, when many states suffered economic recessions, ten states enacted increases in their income taxes, while three states cut income taxes. At the same time, eighteen states increased sales taxes.

TABLE 5. State Taxes per $100 of Personal Income, 1970–87 (1987 dollars)

	Total State Tax	Personal Income	General Sales
1970	$6.29	$1.20	$1.86
1975	$6.68	$1.57	$2.07
1980	$6.78	$1.84	$2.14
1987	$7.02	$2.16	$2.26

Two structural factors have counteracted the federal incentive for state income taxes. States increased their reliance on income taxes by enacting new taxes and increasing rates during the 1960s and early 1970s. The "bracket creep" spurred by the high inflation of the 1970s furthered this reliance as citizens found themselves in higher state tax brackets as their nominal wages rose (Gold 1986; Steuerle 1991). By 1987, state income taxes claimed about the same amount of personal income as did state sales taxes. The inflation of the 1970s thus increased income tax burdens for many individuals and may have tempered any incentive from the Tax Reform Act to further increase state income tax rates in the late 1980s.

A second structural factor that has led states away from income taxation comes from the nature of the 1986 act. Although Congress maintained the deduction for state income taxes, it decreased the value of the deduction by lowering the top marginal income tax rate to 28 percent. In 1981, the top marginal rate was 70 percent, and individuals in that bracket received reductions of seventy cents in federal taxes for every dollar paid in state income taxes. With the 1986 changes, these same persons received federal tax offsets of only twenty-eight cents for every dollar in state taxes and lost much of the exportability or transferability of their state tax liabilities (Gold 1990). Although the 1986 Tax Reform Act advantaged persons paying state income taxes relative to persons paying sales taxes, income taxpayers lost some cushioning that had previously been a part of the federal tax structure. For most taxpayers, this loss amounted to less than 10 percent of their tax liabilities (Courant and Gramlich 1991).

In the next section, I offer case studies of legislators' responses to the symbolic politics of income taxes. I begin with the politics of income taxes in states that have no income tax. In these states, legislators run against the federal income tax and differentiate themselves from their national counterparts by proclaiming that they do not tax citizens' incomes. I then detail the policy initiatives and trade-offs in four states—New Jersey, Mississippi, Michigan, and Vermont—where substantial tax changes have taken place. In Michigan and Mississippi, legislators sought explicit alternatives to obvious income taxes in more obscure sales taxes. In New Jersey, Republican legislators supported Governor Whitman's efforts to reduce income tax rates by one-quarter, although such reductions imply vertical transferability will become relevant as fewer state dollars imply less state assistance to local school districts. In Vermont, the Democratic-controlled House of Representatives bucked the national trend, rejected an income tax cut, and cut the sales tax rate instead. However, Vermont tax politics resulted in state representatives voting to retain the current sales tax rate to fund property tax relief programs—a subject I consider in chapter 5. Finally, I offer two examples of how the symbolic politics of taxation generated largely symbolic political responses in Colorado and New York. In these states, representatives touted rather marginal tax reductions as proof that they were committed to lower taxes, although some argued that the specific nature of the tax reductions could be counterproductive for revenues or economic growth.

Legislators and Taxes: The Quandary of Governing

State legislators find themselves in a quandary when it comes to taxes. The threat of tax revolts and electoral defeat limits state legislators' opportunities to raise taxes without high political costs (Berry and Berry 1992). Conversely, constitutional mandates for balanced state budgets occasion elected officials to periodically confront the unpopular prospects of raising taxes and cutting state services. Thus, legislators have come to seek the least objectionable revenue increases (i.e., sales taxes) while seeking political favor by reducing, however modestly, more obvious and objectionable taxes (i.e., income taxes). In addition to calculations about their own constituents' response to tax changes, representatives must consider how various interest groups will likely mobilize for or against tax proposals. In the case of progressive tax proposals, representatives can likely assume that those whom the proposal most affects will be the same voters with the most resources available to mobilize against the proposal.

There are two important questions affecting the understanding of subnational politics and federalism. The first question is why state policymakers trade one tax for another even when such a shift is revenue neutral. The second question concerns what consequences can be expected from these shifts. There are consequences for state public policies, for state politics vis-à-vis elected representatives, and for politics that traverse the levels of federalism.

I describe four distinct developments in tax politics.

1. In states without an income tax, the income tax offers a symbol of what is wrong with the federal government.
2. In three case-study states, the income tax has served as either the catalyst for or a major determinant of substantial policy changes.
3. Vermont may be considered the exception that proves the rule.

Liberal representatives enacted a sales tax decrease, rejected an income tax cut, and later voted to retain the current sales tax because they wanted to fund property tax relief programs.

4. In Colorado and New York, politicians have offered largely symbolic responses to demands for tax relief.

No-Income-Tax States

In the three states with no personal income taxes—Florida, Tennessee, and Washington—the influence of symbolic politics was clear. Among forty-one legislators, thirty cited citizen disdain for the federal income tax as the reason they either could not support an income tax or did not envision that the state would adopt such a tax. This latter group typically supported an income tax as a matter of policy but opposed it publicly for political reasons. Table 6 details legislators' positions on state income taxes and their observations about why the tax would not be adopted in their states.

The table indicates that representatives identified several reasons for citizens' disdain for income taxes. Among proponents and opponents of an income tax, nearly two-thirds of the representatives cited the federal income tax as the impetus behind citizens' opposition to state income taxes. Income tax opponents were marginally more likely to cite distrust of politicians as a reason for anti–income tax sentiments than were propo-

TABLE 6.   Legislators' Reasons Why an Income Tax Will Not Be Adopted

Percentage of legislators in Florida, Tennessee, and Washington suggesting primary reasons why their state will not adopt an income tax.

	Personal Position	
	Favor (N = 21)	Oppose (N = 19)
Symbol of federal tax	62	74
Distrust of politicians	38	53
Deserves-to-pay principle	5	32
Obscurability of the sales tax	62	21

$N = 40$ (Washington = 14; Tennessee = 13; Florida = 13).

nents. Conversely, proponents believed the obscurability of the sales tax encouraged its acceptance, particularly in comparison to the more obvious income tax.

Citizen distrust of politicians manifests itself in the symbol of the income tax. As a reason for opposing income taxes, representatives mentioned distrust of politicians second only to citizens' disdain for the federal income tax. Forty-five percent of legislators in the no-income-tax states and 25 percent in the five income tax states suggested that their support for alternative taxes resulted in part from citizen disdain for politicians.

Tennessee. Tennessee offers the most striking example of a case where traditional economic and political considerations could lead legislators to support an income tax, yet the political symbolism of the income tax overrides these influences. Of thirteen legislators interviewed, eleven agreed that the state loses money to other states because of a lack of reciprocity with its neighbors. Commuters to Tennessee do not pay income taxes in Tennessee, and Tennesseeans remitting income taxes to neighboring states also pay no taxes to Tennessee. These eleven agreed that Tennessee's tax system was regressive and that tax burdens could be shifted away from poor and moderate-income citizens by imposing an income tax and lowering sales taxes. Yet only seven of these eleven legislators publicly supported an income tax, and no legislator thought it likely that the state would adopt the tax by popular referendum. Despite the possibilities for the state to cut tax burdens for a majority of its citizens, to increase revenues by enacting a tax system with reciprocity, and to create a more diversified, dependable tax base, nearly all legislators rationalized either their inactivity toward or their opposition to an income tax on the grounds that citizens hate the federal income tax and distrust elected officials with income tax revenues. As one legislator mentioned, "I could support it as a matter of tax equity because I have a very working-class district, but they'd vote me out before I could explain the benefits of it. They wouldn't believe me, and it would get nowhere. It's just too hot for them to handle."

As a result of not having an income tax, Tennessee legislators enjoyed the political benefit of being able to run against a federal tax and of distinguishing themselves from their national counterparts in Congress—a benefit about which many expressed relief in 1994. Conversely, legislators perceived implicit political costs from not being able to offer tax rebates or reductions to citizens regardless of economic conditions. More objectively, legislators both supporting and opposing income tax proposals recognized objective losses in terms of jobs and fiscal-drain issues resulting from Tennessee's almost singular reliance on its sales tax.

Florida. A state's current tax system often shapes any efforts at tax reform and the changes legislators contemplate in financing their services. In Florida, all of the legislators interviewed discussed the state's numerous sales tax exemptions on more than 150 categories of merchandise and more than one thousand specific items. Legislators argued that before they could ask their constituents to vote for an income tax, these exemptions would have to be eliminated, with the possible exception of the food exemption. But even the current exemption for food is complicated in Florida. As a rather colorful legislator explained,

> Well, yes, we exempt food, but then you get into a discussion of "What is food?" If you're buying shrimp, for example, they're supposed to ask you at the cash register, "Are you going to eat that?" and if you are, then okay, it's food and it's untaxed. But if you're going to use if for fishing bait then they're supposed to tax it since it's now a recreational item, unless you promise to only eat the fish and not use it for any trophy purpose, in which case the shrimp is then considered a necessity for food production and then it's once again untaxed, but you have to be a professional fisherman for that. Now remember we're talking about a $4.50 an hour cashier here, having to be an expert on tax law.

Florida's other recent effort to enlarge its tax base ended in failure when Governor Robert Martinez at first indicated support for a services tax in 1987 and then led the fight to repeal it. In 1986 the Florida legislature extended the sales tax to a variety of services, including retail services (e.g., haircuts and home repairs) and professional services (e.g., accounting and advertising). This legislation became effective in 1987. Professional groups opposed to the tax suggested that it would cripple Florida's service-driven economy. Advertisers used their position in media markets to mount a campaign for repeal (Francis 1988). One legislator recalled the advertisements from the campaign:

> The ad agencies bought their own time, and they'd have a metronome ticking away on the screen for fifteen seconds, and then a voice-over would come on and say, "Right now you could be watching a com-

mercial for hemorrhoid cream, but all you get is this lousy ticking sound." Now, you'd never think that would have led to a successful effort to repeal the services tax. Hell, it made me think about doubling it, but the governor took off and flipped, so we did away with it.

This representative and several colleagues argued that had the governor not retreated, the furor would have dissipated in six months and the state's revenue position would have been much stronger both during the recent recession and in 1994, when calls for new prison spending and health-care reform led a new governor and legislators to seek additional taxes or the elimination of existing spending programs.

The 1986 experience in Florida indicates that powerful interest groups can successfully oppose and roll back obscure taxes such as the Florida services tax. Both the media campaign and the governor's decision not to support the tax he proposed contributed to the legislature's decision to cut its losses and abandon the tax without testing whether voters would penalize them for it despite any fiscal benefits it may have provided.

Washington.   In contrast to Florida, legislators in Washington felt their refusal to enact an income tax left them unable to reform the state's highly unpopular business and occupation (B and O) tax. The state assesses the B and O tax on employers based on gross receipts, with rates varying according to business or professional category. Twelve of fourteen Washington legislators complained that the B and O tax was regressive and depressed economic growth, but they also argued that its dependability compensated for fluctuations in their 8 percent sales tax. One legislator recognized that Washingtonians had a compounding problem. By relying on a regressive and cyclical sales tax, legislators found it necessary to seek a dependable revenue source. Because an income tax has not been a viable option, legislators have chosen a regressive, obscure, but dependable business tax. Consequently, Washington ranks highest among all states in terms of the percentage of income it taxes from the poorest fifth of its citizens (McIntyre et al. 1991).[4]

As in Florida, Washington legislators generally believed that the state might seek alternatives to an income tax if revenues fell far short of spending. Although six Democrats openly supported an income tax, none expected an income tax to be adopted by popular referendum. Most believed the state probably would attempt to increase revenues by enacting a value-added tax or by expanding the sales tax base to cover services in addition to merchandise. Proposals for either value-added or service taxes enjoyed bipartisan support.

In Florida and Washington, the revenue needs justifying an income tax are less compelling than they are in Tennessee. Nonetheless, legislators worried that they served constituents poorly by maintaining regressive tax systems. Several Washington representatives voluntarily identified their state's distinction of taxing more than 15 percent of the poorest fifth of Washingtonians' income in state sales and local property taxes (see McIntyre et al. 1991). In both Florida and Washington, Republicans and Democrats alike discussed the state's inability to fund education, crime, and transportation programs. They ascribed these limitations to their states' limited tax systems.

Among the three no-income-tax states, the influence of the federal income tax was evident in the legislators' perceptions. The perception that constituents would reject an income tax and punish legislators who supported one left few legislators willing to commit much political capital to promoting one. In these states the a priori condition that an income tax is off the table shapes policy agendas and decisions about how to finance public services. For representatives in Washington, Florida, and Tennessee, the potential political mobilization and costs resulting from the enactment of an income tax were simply too high to risk political capital. Considering the repeated failure of income tax proposals in Tennessee and Washington, representatives suggested that unless enactment was assured they would refrain from supporting such a tax for fear of incurring political losses for a failed proposal. Ironically, even if passage were assured, these legislators feared that the political costs of enactment would be high and would jeopardize their careers. Whereas in other states the movement away from an income tax may be unidirectional, decisions about how to finance services and how to change taxes become more complicated.

Substantial-Change States

At the same time that states have sought to decrease income taxes, they have raised sales taxes. Why would legislators trade one tax for another? The answer is that shifting taxes allows legislators to address policy problems and respond to the political demand for income tax relief. Facing education-policy problems, Michigan and Mississippi representatives opted to increase state responsibility for locally administered education programs to address growing disparities in localities' abilities to fund schools. In New Jersey, the converse transpired. Garden State legislators promoted a state income tax cut, and many expect the state to be less capable of assisting localities in providing services despite court rulings mandating that the state government provide "equal education" throughout New Jersey's school districts.[5]

Mississippi.   Mississippi legislators assembled a supermajority to pass a one-cent increase in the state sales tax in 1992, raising the rate from 6 to 7 percent. Eighteen months later, the same legislators debated two proposals to reduce state income taxes. Many of the legislators supported the sales tax increase and the income tax proposals or other income tax reductions, arguing that citizens accepted—in some cases, demanded—the sales tax increase because the House and Senate earmarked the marginal revenue for education.

When legislators enacted the sales tax increase, the state still felt the effects of the 1990 recession, and casino gambling had yet to generate revenues. With its economy expanding and riverboat gambling producing a $300 million general fund surplus in 1994, the governor proposed two income tax reductions that would cost the state $68 million annually. He did not propose changing the sales tax despite his veto of the 1992 increase, which two-thirds majorities in both legislative chambers voted to override.

For legislators, the decision to increase taxes in 1992 focused on the need to increase education funding. Eleven of fourteen representatives interviewed eventually supported the increase, although one had initially opposed it because he preferred increasing income tax rates. Most legislators felt that the benefits of providing more assistance to schools outweighed the political costs of voting for a tax increase. House members also reported that their constituents said they could support a sales tax increase but not an income tax increase. As one legislator explained,

> We had a situation where we couldn't get the votes in the House for an income tax increase. If we had them, we'd have lost a lot of seats in that election two months later. Then you'd face repeal of what we fought for. So it came down to either biting the bullet to get two-thirds for the sales tax or mandat[ing] school districts provide the services we were going to provide. . . . The problem with doing the mandates is

that it doesn't address the issue of getting money to poor districts so they can provide the services. You can't ask a Delta district to go over 10 mills on its property tax. So sure, it was regressive, but I think that's outweighed by the state's ability to redistribute the money to poor districts.

In 1994 Governor Kirk Fordice proposed increasing the personal exemption for the state's income tax from $6,500 to $9,500 and exempting senior citizens from state income taxes. Interestingly, the proponents of these tax changes were conservative Republicans seeking to reduce taxes and liberal Democrats who saw these changes as opportunities to make the state's tax system more progressive. Moderate Republicans and Democrats opposed to the tax cuts cited the state's ill-fated 1979 tax cut, which was followed by fourteen years of deficit projections and various reductions in state spending.

Opponents of Governor Fordice's proposals feared that a repeat of the 1979 tax reductions would result in unpopular spending reductions for years after the benefits of a tax decrease abated. Several Democrats opposed exempting senior citizens on the grounds that retirees with pensions were not overtaxed in Mississippi and that other groups, such as working parents, should be considered for tax preferences along with senior citizens. Nonetheless, legislators found it hard to turn down proposals from a conservative governor offering tax reductions and a more progressive tax system. One liberal legislator from a relatively poor district said, "I don't see how I can vote against Fordice's proposal—it offers tax relief to a lot of people in my district. It may bankrupt the state, and they won't like it when we cut education, but it's a very hard vote to say no to."

Ultimately, the legislature compromised and passed the income tax exemption for senior citizens and defeated the change in the personal exemption. According to a member of the Fordice administration, moderate Democrats and a few Republicans voted down the personal exemption change because of their concerns about revenue dependability and because of the state's experience with the 1979 tax cut. The majority of Republicans and a few liberal Democrats supported both tax reductions.

Comparing Mississippi's sales tax increase and its competing income tax proposals in 1994 demonstrates how difficult it can be for individual representatives to translate their governing principles into public policy. All but one Democrat and a few of the Republican legislators recognized that the income tax was the best way to tax citizens according to the ability-to-pay principle. The need to assemble a two-thirds majority to override the governor's veto and the resistance to impose an unfunded mandate on local school districts generated support for the relatively regressive sales tax increase to increase education funding. Concerns about revenue dependability made the governor's most progressive revenue proposal, the three-thousand-dollar increase in the personal exemption, prohibitively expensive. Horizontal tax competition with other southeastern states and the targeted benefits of the seniors' exemption (which made it less expensive than the general exemption increase) created the situation in which legislators set aside some of their equity concerns and voted to create particular benefits.

There was greater support for the seniors' exemption because its Democratic and Republican proponents viewed it as a component of economic development policy. Ways and Means Committee members hoped the seniors' exemption would attract relatively wealthy retirees to the state and cited estimates by the state revenue department that the state would recoup foregone income tax revenues with increased sales tax revenues in three to seven years. During the debate on the measure, legislators pointed out that a number of other southeastern states either exempted pension incomes from their income taxes or were considering proposals to do so. In this respect, the proposal became an implicit development policy as well as a competitive response to neighboring states' income tax policy changes. With respect to development, legislators hoped that an influx of retirees would create new jobs in construction and various service industries.

Mississippi representatives have thus found that the timing and packaging of tax proposals affects their position on the proposal. Perceptions of widespread support for education spending led legislators to vote for a sales tax increase. The need to assemble a two-thirds majority to override the governor's veto along with concerns about the variation in resources among local districts led legislators to seek a sales tax increase rather than an income tax increase or mandates on local districts. Less than two years later, a good economic climate and new revenues from riverboat gambling created a situation in which the Republican governor could propose progressive income tax reductions. Although the proposals may have been popular with many voters, some legislators still opposed the changes, fearing the state had not established sufficiently dependable revenues to warrant major tax reductions that might be rescinded later.

Michigan. Representatives in the Great Lakes state discovered two things about tax changes. First, when given the choice, voters would not cut taxes irresponsibly. On two occasions when voters perceived that property tax reduction referenda would provide no alternative or inadequate funding for primary and secondary education, they rejected the proposals. Second, tax proposals could be presented in such a way as to insulate representatives from the political costs associated with major tax changes. By using Michigan's referendum process, representatives made voters responsible for choosing the level and method of tax reform. When voters overwhelmingly enacted a sales tax increase and rejected an income tax increase, they indicated to legislators their strong desire for obscure taxes, and they let legislators avoid having to decide how to relieve voters of obvious and highly unpopular property tax burdens.

Michigan legislators presented voters with a referendum designed to alleviate property taxes and growing financial inequities among school districts. Regardless of whether voters approved or rejected the referendum, Proposal A, property taxes would be reduced. If voters rejected Proposal A, a statutory alternative crafted by legislators would have become law. In addition to lowering property taxes, Proposal A increased the state sales tax from 4 to 6 percent, whereas the statutory alternative replaced lost property tax revenues by increasing the state income tax. Table 7 provides

TABLE 7.   Elements of Michigan's Proposal A

Proposal A	Statutory Alternative
Reduced basic millage to 8 mills on homestead property	Basic millage at 12 mills
Raised sales tax to 6 percent	Retained 4 percent sales tax
Lowered income tax from 4.6 percent to 4.4 percent	Raised income tax to 6.0 percent
No change in the personal exemption	Raised personal exemption from $2,100 to $3,000
Raised tobacco tax from 25 to 75 cents per pack	No change in tobacco tax
Lowered single business tax from 2.75 percent to 2.35 percent	No change in single business tax

a comparison of Proposal A and the statutory alternative. Voters approved Proposal A by a 40 percent margin.

Legislators addressed a growing policy problem with Proposal A. With increased state sales tax revenues, legislators and the governor reformulated the state's primary and secondary education financing and offered greater assistance to schools with moderate property values but more modest income profiles—the districts in which voters had opposed millage increases, thus forcing administrators to close schools as early as March because of a lack of funds.

Legislators both opposed to and in favor of Proposal A noted that its authors designed it to be politically attractive. The statutory alternative distinguished it from previous tax reform proposals, which had offered property tax relief without alternative financing. Consequently, citizens did not have to wonder how their schools would be funded if they voted in favor of property tax relief. Michigan legislators emphasized that the proposal not only addressed the property tax issue but also decreased a highly visible tax while raising a more obscure incremental tax. All of the opponents and proponents of the proposal suggested that the obscurability of the sales tax made it preferable to income and property taxes.

The modest reduction in the income tax rate meant that the governor and legislative proponents could campaign for Proposal A as a tax decrease for all citizens regardless of whether they owned property. Several proponents noted that the statutory alternative decreased income taxes only for those with low incomes.[6] For representatives, the political benefits started with their option to exercise the referendum process, by which they shifted the responsibility for the tax change to voters. The second benefit came from proposing a statutory alternative that ensured relief from property taxes, and the question for voters then became one of choosing between their own preferences for tax progressivity or tax obscurability. By an overwhelming margin, they chose obscurability. For representatives, the process was fail-safe in that it addressed a growing policy problem—inequitable and in some cases inadequate property taxes to fund local schools—and voters held the onus for deciding how to fix the problem.

Two proponents and one opponent suggested that the cigarette tax was really more for political packaging than for policy purposes. The designers of the proposal anticipated tobacco companies would vigorously oppose Proposal A and that a citizen backlash against their advertising would increase chances for approval. One proponent noted that it was hard in Michigan to discredit the teachers' union, the Michigan Education Association, but that having the tobacco lobby and the union stand out as the two principal interest-group opponents of the proposal was "a unique opportunity to associate a generally supported group, the MEA, with a group most believe to be lower than a snake's belly, the cigarette people."

In Michigan and Mississippi, representatives offered no reduction in services but substantial tax changes. However, these changes contained elements of compromise resulting from the politics of income taxes and citizen preferences for obscure taxes. In Mississippi, representatives imposed a regressive statewide tax increase to provide more education funding to poorer school districts. Yet the districts that would gain the most in services would pay disproportionately in taxes, although not as much as if they had had to fund services with local property taxes. The following year, legislators had the opportunity to make the state's income tax more progressive, thereby offsetting the regressivity of the previous tax increase for some citizens. Other legislators perceived the income tax changes as an attempt by the governor to bankrupt the state and precipitate future service cuts. Legislators thus opposed the income tax reductions out of concern that their constituents' benefit/tax ratios would suffer in the long run.

In Michigan most legislators viewed both Proposal A and its statutory alternative as a means to increase their citizens benefit/tax ratios. The cleavage among legislators resulted from their views on whether constituents should pay for state assumption of education funding according to income or consumption. The voters of Michigan clearly preferred the incremental, albeit regressive, sales tax increase to the more obvious income tax increase, which could have been deducted from their federal income taxes.

New Jersey.   Shifting among taxes can suggest a major shift in the direction of government. Governor Christine Whitman pledged to reduce income tax rates by 25 percent over three years. Several legislators pointed out, however, that few voters know that under New Jersey's laws, state income tax revenues are dedicated to assisting local governments. Consequently, many citizens may find themselves paying higher local property taxes. All ten legislators interviewed agreed that local governments would either raise taxes or reduce spending. The four Democrats interviewed supported the governor's initial proposal for a 5 percent cut in 1994. They believed the state could replace lost local aid by shifting revenue out of its own departments, such as higher education. These four either opposed or had apprehensions about further income tax reductions if such reductions led to decreases in state assistance to localities. One Republican from a traditionally urban Democratic district predicated his support for further tax cuts on the pledge he felt the governor had made to not harm localities financially because of the state's tax reduction. Two Republicans claimed that state aid to localities should be cut so citizens could better understand exactly which governments provided which services and at what costs. They contended that forcing local officials to make tough decisions would enhance the accountability of government and end citizen complaints about waste and inefficiency in Trenton.

In addition to supporting an initial tax cut and having concerns about future cuts, assembly members in New Jersey leaned in favor of relying more heavily on the sales tax in the future. One member of the Republican leadership commented that he was not worried about having to raise sales taxes if the income tax reductions created revenue shortfalls:

> *Assembly Member:* I think we acted a bit early by rolling back the sales tax increase Florio put on, but politically we had pledged to do it in '92, so we did. Actually, that worked out well because Christie got to run on the income tax, then, and if we had rolled back that increase she couldn't have run on a sales tax decrease because it's more complex and doesn't crystallize voter thoughts. . . . Now, if we run short [of money], I think we could go back and ask for a sales tax increase, particularly if we tie it to property tax relief and education. In fact, several of my constituents have come up to me and asked, "Why don't you put that penny back on the sales tax?"
>
> *GB:* Really?
>
> *Assembly Member:* Yes, it's not a groundswell, but they like the sales tax. Everybody pays it, it helps with education, and it's not the income tax.

In New Jersey, legislators and the governor were not able to offer tax proposals similar to those in Michigan and Mississippi. Whereas legislators in the latter states offered tax changes with no decrease in services, legislators in New Jersey knew that tax reductions implied either state or local service reductions. Thus the question of what happens to benefit/tax ratios becomes a function of which services the legislature reduces or eliminates, which constituents utilize those services, and who benefits from tax reductions. Republicans and Democrats overwhelmingly agreed that higher-income individuals would benefit from the income tax reductions since their marginal 7 percent tax rate would be reduced to 5.2 percent under Governor Whitman's proposal. What was less known outside the legislature is that under its original implementing legislation, the income tax is dedicated to financial assistance to localities. Localities will bear the burden of deciding which of their services to cut or which taxes to increase to make up for lost state funds. Consequently, assembly members from poorer urban districts worried that their constituents would be made worse off by the state income tax reduction—their benefit/tax ratios would decline—but would not make the connections among local service reductions, property tax increases, and a state income tax cut. Legislators from wealthier districts defended the potential benefits of the tax reduction and said localities should face the same difficult choices the state faces. They also argued that giving less money to localities would allow citizens more local determination of which services to offer in their communities.

In several states, income taxes became entangled in significant policy decisions. In these states, legislators were unified in their desire to provide some sort of relief from income or property taxes and debated how to package such relief politically and simultaneously address other policy problems. In both Michigan and Mississippi, legislators felt they could campaign for sales tax increases but not income tax increases, and indeed, many legislators advocated income tax reductions. In New Jersey, nearly all legislators supported a 5 percent cut in income tax rates, and many supported further rate reductions. Those who were not prepared to support an additional 20 percent reduction cited their concerns about localities in their assembly districts losing state aid. In all three states, income tax policy has played a central role in the development of other policies—education in Mississippi and Michigan and local aid in New Jersey.

Vermont.   There is one exception to the move away from cutting income taxes, and it involves decisions about cutting taxes, not raising them. Vermont representatives initially voted to cut the state sales tax from 5 to 4 percent but then indefinitely delayed the rate decrease. The additional $33 million in revenue still went for tax relief, but instead of coming from state sales taxes the legislature dedicated the revenues to fully funding Vermont's four property tax-relief programs.

Although the process remained within the legislature, Vermont's experience with tax changes in 1995 was similar to Michigan's in 1994. Legislators perceived greater political benefits if the state assumed greater responsibility for education funding and in turn relied on the relatively obscure sales tax to finance this assumption. In Vermont, the funding for property tax relief was indirect. Vermont legislators voted to retain a higher sales tax to fund various property tax rebates, whereas in Michigan legislators and voters supported a direct trade in which a higher sales tax mandated decreased property tax rates. The marginal sales tax revenue funded tax-relief programs for locally imposed property taxes that in turn funded primary and secondary education.

Liberal Democrats had sought to decrease a relatively regressive tax, but in the current political climate, calling for decreased property taxes and facing irreconcilable differences on how to rationalize the state property tax system, legislators instead chose to continue using the least objectionable of taxes, retail sales, as a means of addressing other political and financial problems.

Symbolic Responses to Symbolic Politics

In the final cluster of states, tax politics does not play a central role in determining the broad policy agenda or in eliminating policy options, as it did in the no-income-tax states. Tax politics also does not have a major role in policy development. In Colorado and New York, the symbolism of tax politics has been met with pro forma, but not trivial, responses from citizens and legislators.

In Colorado, a series of ballot initiatives regarding tax capitations and reductions demonstrated voters' antitax mood, but most representatives felt that the voters' actions were symbolic responses to federal taxes and that providing outlets for such citizen sentiment created latitude for legislators and local officials to sell other, more pressing revenue concerns to their citizens. In November 1992 citizens approved Amendment 1, which mandates that all further tax increases are subject to citizen approval. Simultaneously, citizens rejected Amendment 6, which would have provided additional funding for public education by raising the state sales tax from 3 to 4 percent. In 1993 voters exercised their power under Amendment 1 and elected to end the state's tourism tax and Denver's culture tax. Both taxes were earmarked portions of the 3 percent sales tax.

Legislators generally viewed these citizen actions as largely symbolic revolts against taxes that did little to change the state government's resources. Eight of eleven legislators said they felt that their constituents were taking advantage of the state-provided outlet to express their disdain for federal taxes as much as for state taxes.

In New York, the governor, assembly members, and state senators forged compromises during the winter and spring of 1994 to offer about $80 million in tax relief to low-income individuals and corporations. The Democratic governor and Democrat-controlled House promoted an earned-income tax credit for low-wage workers with children, while the Republican-controlled state senate promoted cuts in business taxes. The eventual compromise contained an earned-income tax credit for families with annual incomes below $37,000 and a reduction in the corporate-profits tax rate. Two points deserve mention. First, neither cut had a dramatic fiscal effect on New York's $37 billion annual budget. During the negotiations, policymakers reduced the earned-income tax credit as a percentage of income while increasing the scope of taxpayers eligible. A senior member of the House Ways and Means Committee told me it was no coincidence that about half of all families in New York would be eligible for a credit: "It's nice to say you cut half the people's taxes. It sure beats a third, even if the bottom quarter isn't getting the help they need."

All eight legislators interviewed in New York agreed that the corporate tax cuts were receiving much more attention than the income tax credit from both politicians and the media. Most legislators ascribed this situation to the public perception that business tax cuts would create jobs and that the assembly was sending a signal to businesses that the Empire State was becoming more business friendly. Legislators said this tax change was largely symbolic in terms of how probusiness New York would become and in terms of which businesses would benefit. One assembly member detailed how the same cut in corporate-profits taxes could have been used to eliminate gross-receipts taxes on commercial gas and electric bills that businesses find onerous regardless of their profitability. A second legislator pointed out that several of the state's largest corporations had deferments on their state income taxes well into the decade because they could roll over losses from the 1990 recession to the current tax year. Consequently, the state would not necessarily assist businesses in retaining more profits than would have otherwise been the case. The assembly member noted,

> If we had cut the gross-receipts tax, we'd be out money, no question. But here Cuomo and the senate majority leader can announce a big tax cut that because of deferments, credits, roll forward, and, Christ, actual

losses will cost the treasury not a dime. It's really ingenious. They get the mileage of a tax cut without much consequence on revenues.

In New York, enough legislators emphasized the ability-to-pay principle to gain an earned-income tax credit as part of its 1994 tax-relief package. Senate Republicans emphasized development and reached agreement with Governor Mario Cuomo on a reduction in the corporate-profits tax despite admissions from both Republicans and Democrats that economic development might be better served by reducing utility taxes.

Discussion

Legislators have shifted away from obvious levies, such as property and income taxes, to relatively obscure gross-receipts and sales taxes. Most legislators feel that because citizens pay sales taxes in small albeit frequent increments, they are less objectionable than income taxes. Additionally, consumers pay the tax when purchasing items they want—merchandise that presumably improves their well-being. Most legislators feel political acceptance of sales taxes outweighs the dilemma they present by complicating government accountability.

Legislators' largest overriding concern with respect to the state tax shifts focused on equity. Only three of ninety-seven legislators disagreed with the premise that sales taxes were relatively regressive. Many legislators felt it unfortunate that sales taxes were the first choice of taxes to increase. These representatives reasoned that they provided less for their poorer constituents than they could have or failed to appropriately tax wealthier citizens. But again and again, representatives defended the decision to support sales tax increases and income tax cuts. In Mississippi, the need for a two-thirds majority support to override the governor's veto and concerns about localities' abilities to raise funds via property taxes led to a sales tax increase. Michigan legislators defended their support for Proposal A over the legislative alternative, noting that constituents perceive the sales tax to be more fair than the income tax and that a portion of the sales tax is paid by tourists. A Tennessee legislator even argued that regressive taxation made sense because "while rich people make the sacrifices necessary to save their money, poor people don't. If we tax them disproportionately, it's like getting them to invest their money—even in something as inefficient as government. And the more we tax them, the more services we can provide the poor, and the higher the return on their investment becomes."

The tax changes demonstrated that in the federal tax politics of the mid-1990s, the shift to obscurability created several potential political benefits. Representatives in Michigan, New Jersey, and New York could claim they were cutting income taxes, however modestly, in the wake of two federal income tax increases. Vermont representatives could use slack in their sales tax revenues to offer additional relief from obvious, and varied, local property taxes. Representatives in Tennessee, Florida, and Washington could use the absence of state income taxes to differentiate themselves from their federal counterparts. These responses go beyond the structural vertical-base competition created by the 1990 and 1993 federal income tax increases, which affected upper-income people. The substantial tax changes in Michigan, Mississippi, and New Jersey go far beyond what legislators would have enacted to offset the federal income tax increases of 1990 and 1993. These tax politics demonstrate that states will engage in wholesale policy changes motivated by their own politics and policy challenges.

State representatives perceive that the shift away from income taxes may leave them without a relatively dependable, broad-based revenue source, although they differ on the consequences. In Michigan, New York, and Washington, legislators surmised that their states would continue to be saddled with unpopular gross-receipts taxes on businesses to provide dependable revenue sources. Repeatedly, I heard expressions to the effect of, "We'll soon have only a two-legged stool. So, much as you might hate that second leg, you can't change it, because you have no way to stand if that leg goes too." In Colorado, Florida, Mississippi, and Tennessee, legislators bemoaned their state's erratic revenue fluctuations. Some believed that the state could compensate by establishing greater reserve funds and more stable spending practices, but most believed the state governments would continue their traditions of feast and famine—increasing spending dramatically during economic expansions only to cut it all the more drastically during recessions. One legislator in Tennessee noted that with his state's reliance on consumption taxes there were no means by which the state could rebate surplus revenues to citizens, as it could with income tax rebates.

Further complicating state politics is local tax politics. Legislators perceived continued citizen resistance to property taxes and thus sought to alleviate citizens' tax burdens without sacrificing funding for basic services and particularly for education. Such resistance to the primary source of local revenues has left state legislators in a bind in which they face pressure not to enact income taxes because of federal politics, to assume greater responsibility for locally administered services, and to provide tax relief for middle-income individuals who protest property taxation. Consequently, state legislators are left to seek relatively obscure revenues and taxes that meet the least public resistance. For most states this situation has meant an increased reliance on the sales tax.

In the short term the "no new income taxes" philosophy that pervades state politics is likely to mean that few states will engage in sweeping income tax reform designed to make generally regressive state tax systems progressive. By blocking such reform, citizens will continue to pay obscure regressive taxes, and thus state governments will continue to operate under the benefits-received principle. Moreover, an unwillingness on the part of legislators to lead fights for tax reform will hamper their efforts to attain other collective goals, such as economic development. For example, in Washington, Michigan, and New York businesses will continue to pay gross-receipts taxes. Most legislators believe that these taxes depress job creation but have few alternative revenue sources outside of personal and corporate income taxes.

Another possible consequence of the abandonment of income as a large and stable tax base may be that the intergovernmental competition among subnational governments posited by Peterson (1981) and Dye (1990) may shift to a vertical competition among federal, state, and local governments. As governments compete for these revenue bases, they may increasingly find themselves unable to cooperate with one another in financing endeavors as they have in the past twenty years. Subsequently, disparities in the abilities of localities to provide services may increase and exacerbate differences in the benefits citizens receive from governments.

An unintended consequence of an increase in sales taxes is that regardless of voter sentiments, state tax revenues may no longer keep pace with economic or population growth. Several Washington legislators noted that state tax revenue growth corresponded poorly to economic growth during the 1980s despite impressive employment and income growth fueled by the defense buildup and the expansion of computer-related industries. As one legislator said,

> We were probably in the top ten states as far as economic growth, but the state government lagged and has had to increase tax rates upward. Part of it was to alleviate growing discrepancies in property tax bases, but the main problem was that our tax system gave us no way to

access that income growth. If you have no income tax, all the income growth in the world only helps you as much as people who spend money in the state on things other than food, and as people get wealthier they travel more, and we lose to places like L. L. Bean, for God's sake.

The unintended consequence of the current shift in tax policy may be that states will find themselves unable to generate the revenue needed to meet demands for services that expand with state economies and population. As interstate sales via mail order and other means continue to expand along with the service sector of the economy, states may need to either expand sales tax bases into interstate sales and services or return to taxing income to have taxes that are responsive to economic changes.

Conclusion

Looking to the future, one can reasonably predict that the politics of cutting state income taxes cannot go on forever, if only because tax rates have a lower bound of zero. At that point, the politics of income taxation will have run its course. Politicians at all levels of government may emphasize principles that lead them to again promote income taxes. However, states will likely continue to grapple with tough tax questions, and recent experience indicates that legislators will contend with the perceived benefit/tax ratio changes as much as they will with objective changes in spending and taxes.

Overall, the movement away from income taxes at the state level moves states away from a quasi-Lindahl tax system and thus implies that consumer surplus is lower for many constituents than it could be if states relied more on progressive tax policies. It is ironic that the federal government's reliance on a modestly progressive income tax and regressive wage tax constrains states from enacting more progressive tax policies. This situation leaves states with few options other than to seek to enlarge existing tax bases, limit services, and rely on obscure, regressive, but revenue-yielding sales and business taxes. Among these options, pursuing economic development has become universal, and legislators view it as the most desirable means to increase revenues. I consider this subject in the next chapter.

Chapter 5

Tax and Spend or Spending Taxes—Economic Development in the States

Although legislators differ on issues pertaining to the means by which to finance government, they are united in their pursuit of enlarging tax bases via economic development. Since the 1970s, state officials have substantially increased their attention to economic development (Eisinger 1988; Brace 1993; Beyle 1983). Thirty of the legislators in this study (23 percent) either described themselves as specializing in economic development or considered economic development an important legislative priority. The half dozen representatives who resisted discussing economic development because they lacked expertise nonetheless described in detail their preferences for particular components of economic development policies.

There is considerable evidence detailing various state economic development efforts (Brace 1993; Dye 1990) and the efficacy of these policies (Courant 1994), yet less is known about how legislators and legislatures produce development policies and why they choose one set of development tools over others. Legislators share the goal of expanding their states' economies and creating new jobs and investment opportunities. They differ on how to pursue this collective goal. Two strategies exemplify legislators' choices between particular-benefits and public-goods strategies.

Economic development policy provides clear cases of representatives deciding between public goods and particular benefits in the pursuit of the same goals—growing economies and expanded tax bases. In addition to legislators' individual preferences for public-goods and particular-benefits strategies to enhance economic growth, state policy histories, citizen participation, and horizontal tax competition among states influence the development of state economic development policy.

The economic development case studies from Tennessee, Mississippi,

New York, Colorado, and Washington and the individual interview data enhance the understanding of the variance among state development processes and illuminate the roles of state policy histories and policy interactions, opportunities for citizen participation, and intergovernmental relations. Despite empirical evidence that state development efforts may expend more marginal resources than they attract or generate (Courant 1994), most legislators believe these policies are worthwhile. This chapter offers an understanding of legislators' perceptions about interstate competition for employers. Although other studies have offered considerable evidence for interstate competition, few have reported directly on legislators' views about interstate competition and legislative responses to it (Eisinger 1988; Brace 1993).

Representatives are aware of and contend with the relationships and linkages among different policy areas. In the case studies of New Jersey, New York, and Washington, legislators expressed frustrations that general tax policies mitigated state development efforts. This "paradox of development" is not apparent if one views state economic development policy isolated from other state tax and spending policies.

Both public-goods and particular-benefits strategies provide political advantages for elected officials. Legislators can point to public goods such as community colleges and infrastructure improvements and claim credit for bringing the particular benefits, or positive externalities, of such goods to their districts. More directly, when particular benefits such as tax abatements or financial underwriting result in a state attracting a specific employer, legislators can claim credit for specific jobs in their districts.

The avenues of federalism available to state legislators for economic development are largely those between states and localities. And it is on these state and local avenues that the creative politics regarding development policies take place. State legislatures enact tax policies that circumscribe and preempt local tax policies. They rationalize that foregone local revenues can be offset by larger revenue bases. Alternatively, state governments may provide funding for employment and training at local or regional community colleges or funding for roads and infrastructure that will benefit municipalities. With respect to specific tax policies, state legislatures in Florida and Mississippi have used their incorporation powers either to create new special-district governments or to abate local taxes to lure employers.

To the extent that avenues of federalism run between the federal and state governments, they assume characteristics more akin to back alleys than to broad, clearly defined avenues. The lack of a national federal development policy has left states considerable latitude for developing their own policies (Eisinger 1988). In addition, federal spending, particularly defense spending, has implicitly influenced state development by funneling federal resources into specific states. The states have in turn used Department of Defense facilities and their contractors as anchor employers in their efforts to attract various high-technology firms (Schulman 1992; Mintz and Huang 1990; Leib 1992; Young 1993). Substantial federal spending and grants for education and infrastructure assist states in funding development policies (Brace 1993; Schulman 1992). Legislators in Washington, Colorado, Florida, and Massachusetts discussed defense spending's positive influence on their states' economies. In the 1980s their state governments relied on such spending as an economic stabilizer and as an avenue by which they could attract high-technology employers.

Scholars have argued that subnational politicians pursue economic development over and above redistributive policies (Dye 1990; Peterson 1981). For state governments to have sufficient resources to redistribute income or spend money on health and education programs, they must have sufficient tax bases. Consequently, politicians focus on development prior to turning their attention to other functions of government if only because development provides a basis for financing these other functions (Peterson 1981). The competition for employers discourages states from enacting large-scale redistributive tax-and-spending policies lest some states become "magnets" for the poor and other states havens for the wealthy (Peterson and Rom 1990; Dye 1990; Brace 1993; Peterson 1981). State representatives will attend to development because of an internal need to finance government and external competition for revenues.

Should economic development efforts succeed, legislators can increase benefit/tax ratios via two avenues. Enlarged tax bases and fiscal slack created by reduced demand for state services imply that legislators can raise equivalent amounts of revenue at lower tax rates. Legislatures can reduce taxes without decreasing services. Alternatively, legislators can increase funding for programs. Several legislators mentioned that one of the advantages of pursuing economic development was that the state could couple its development efforts with attempts to reduce spending on unpopular income-assistance programs. Both scenarios indicate unequivocal increases in aggregate benefit/tax ratios.

Legislators indicated an interest in three questions. First, what are the explicit costs to the state government from a particular development policy? These costs can be direct expenditures, tax expenditures, or, more implicitly, foregone revenues. Second, what are the implicit costs of a policy? These costs include additional services the state or localities may offer as a consequence of attracting new jobs and citizens. Such costs may include added educational costs or increased pollution-control costs. Third, does a policy enhance a state's comparative advantages or mitigate its relative disadvantages? About one-third of the legislators suggested that promoting relative advantages and lessening disadvantages created more cost-effective development strategies than did tax incentives or spending on education not tied to specific employment.

Representatives can calculate the political benefits of either a public-goods or a particular-benefits development strategy. With public goods, benefits may be more dispersed, but citizens can enjoy the same benefits, such as roads and infrastructure, as potential employers. With particular benefits, representatives can claim credit for specific jobs from specific employers, but the distribution of economic benefits may be much more concentrated than with a public-goods approach. For most states, economic development policies have incorporated elements of both public-goods and particular-benefits strategies, thereby providing legislators with access to benefits in either form.

States rarely initiate development policies contemporaneously. Legislators fine-tune their development efforts in response to changes in their economies and to the national macroeconomy (Brace 1993). The lack of a federal industrial policy, states' tax, education, and infrastructure policies, and states' incorporation powers and their abilities to limit or preempt local taxes create the politics surrounding economic development efforts (Eisinger 1988).

Three questions arise from legislators' proactive support for development policies and their strategic differences in how to pursue a collective goal. First, to what extent can different positions about development policy be accounted for? Second, how do preferences translate into policies? Finally, who stands to benefit from different policies, or what changes in benefit/tax ratios result from such policies?

Legislators' Development Preferences

Legislators divide into three groups with respect to economic development. The first group emphasizes public goods such as education, infrastructure, and, to a lesser extent, health care. The alternative group favors targeting particular benefits in various forms of tax incentives and credits to attract and retain employers. In the middle ground are legislators who emphasize some combination of particular benefits and public goods. These representatives stressed the advantages of having a good education system and adequate infrastructure and suggested that tax incentives for employers were necessary because of interstate competition for employers (Eisinger 1988).

Different development strategies imply different costs and benefits for citizens and employers. Public-goods strategies imply that citizens can take advantage of programs and goods offered by the state. Primary benefits flow not only to employers, who take advantage of new roads or a well-trained workforce, but also to citizens, who have access to infrastructure and education. With a particular-benefits strategy emphasizing employer tax incentives, employers enjoy primary benefits from tax abatements or interest subsidies. Citizens and firms whose tax rates are implicitly higher as a result of an employer tax abatement bear the costs of these benefits (Steuerle 1991; Eisinger 1988). Nonetheless, a particular-benefits strategy implies that primary benefits flow to citizens whose wages increase if a new employer comes to a state and that secondary benefits flow to all citizens as the tax base grows and the demand for state redistributive services declines.

Legislators emphasizing a public-goods strategy suggested that benefits would be available to citizens regardless of whether public goods succeeded in attracting new employers.[1] Citizens could increase their benefit/tax ratios by taking advantage of the educational programs or infrastructure offered—by increasing their consumption of government-provided benefits.

Representatives who focused on employer tax incentives emphasized a particular-benefits strategy. The advantage of this strategy is that the state expends resources only when an employer is attracted to the state. Supporters of this strategy argued that tax incentives were more efficient than education and transportation programs that may or may not produce dividends. In addition, the legislators did not have to worry that citizens would take advantage of education and training programs, only to leave the state for high-wage jobs elsewhere. By tying the benefits to employers, supporters of the tax-incentive strategy argued for an approach they perceived to be more efficient than strategies involving nonexclusionary public goods.

Preferences for economic development policies sort along party lines.

Twenty-three percent of the legislators listing a top priority for economic development emphasized state programs for education and training. Of these eighteen legislators, sixteen were Democrats and two were Republicans. Eighteen legislators (23 percent) said that tax incentives were the best way to foster economic development, and eleven of these legislators were Republicans. There is an important difference between legislators who promoted tax reform and those who promoted tax incentives. Tax incentives are particular tax credits or deductions for new or expanding firms. Employers qualify on an individual basis for these incentives. Tax reforms are broad-based changes in state taxes that affect many, if not all, individuals and businesses in the state. For example, Washington legislators promoted enacting an income tax and eliminating the state business and occupation tax. These legislators supported changes that focused on the totality of the state tax code. Conversely, representatives in Mississippi supported tax incentives, bills allowing ninety-nine-year abatements on county ad valorem taxes. Table 8 further details legislators' priorities for economic development strategies.

Legislators emphasizing education and infrastructure funding promoted a public-goods strategy for economic development, whereas those who emphasized tax incentives preferred a particular-benefits strategy for development (Levin 1987; Fitzgerald 1993). Although education confers particular benefits, I categorize it as a public good for several reasons.

TABLE 8.   Legislators' Primary Emphasis for Economic Development

Policy	Number Giving Policy First Priority			
	Total		Democrats	Republicans
Education	18	(23%)	36%	8%
Tax incentives	18	(23%)	16%	42%
Tax reform	13	(16%)	20%	15%
Infrastructure	11	(14%)	18%	12%
Regulatory changes	10	(12%)	9%	23%
Other[a]	10	(12%)		

N = 80 (49 Democrats and 31 Republicans)

[a]Ten legislators gave individual responses, including quality of life, public-works jobs programs modeled on the WPA, spending reductions, advertising the state, port subsidies, reducing the national capital-gains tax, transforming state parks into golf courses, subsidized housing programs, and a state-sponsored minority set-aside program. Percentages in the second and third columns represent the distribution of responses among Democrats and Republicans who proffered one of the listed priorities.

Representatives indicated a need to finance education such that all citizens would enjoy access to training that would enable them to increase their earnings. No single citizen's use of education or training programs would inhibit another citizen from using similar services. Moreover, representatives in every state discussed offering educational opportunities and experiences to citizens and an increased state role in funding job training. To the extent that education confers particular benefits, legislators can enact policies whereby beneficiaries bear the cost of their particular benefits in tuition payments (i.e., the state can internalize the costs of particular benefits, or positive externalities). Such policies leave the state share of costs at a level consistent with the social benefits accruing from education and training. A well-educated populace may enjoy better health and thus demand fewer public-health services. Furthermore, legislators in nearly every state contended that a well-educated workforce attracted higher-paying employers.

Infrastructure is more clearly a public good than is education. Among legislators who promoted roads, sewers, and environmental projects for economic development, a division existed between those who believed that the state should develop a broad strategy for infrastructure and those who believed that infrastructure funds should be held until a potential employer identified the infrastructure enhancements that would make a site attractive. In the former category, legislators in Tennessee commented on a plan nicknamed the "roads to nowhere program" in which a former committee chairperson convinced his colleagues that if the state built roads and provided utility systems in rural areas, employers would find the state attractive and build plants and facilities. As one Democrat commented,

> You have to give the chairman credit—he had us building four-lane highways going through forests and pastures, and everybody thought he was crazy. At the time, we were so broke those programs were basically public works, but the chairman kept saying, "If we build it they will come" [laughs], like that movie that came out a few years later. And John was right, because ten years later we have Saturn, Nissan, GE, and all their suppliers around here. It was a strategy nobody would have really banked on, but it says, "We're willing to give you what you need to do business from here." What will a tax incentive do for you if you can't get to a rail line or . . . a loading dock?

In Michigan, Massachusetts, New Jersey, and New York, legislators emphasized spending money not on new roads but on existing, decaying infrastructure. Concerns about infrastructure investment emanated from threats that existing business would exit or close. Several representatives recognized a tension between assisting manufacturers, many of which are in declining industries, and helping newer high-technology firms in health care, financial services, and communications. The latter firms typically have required less traditional physical infrastructure and more employee training and education. When their economies declined, several legislators felt they were in a catch-22 situation: if they did not assist the remaining industry in their state, the tax bases would erode precipitously and impede the ability to invest in education and training programs necessary to attract new firms. Yet by investing in declining industries, representatives pursued a course that constrained their ability to attract new industry.

Many legislators discussed paradoxical or contradictory components of economic development strategies. Tax incentives, education, and infra-structure promoted growth, yet other policies impeded it. This problem became apparent when legislators argued that the best development policy for their states would be overall tax reform. Democrats in Tennessee, Washington, New Jersey, and New York argued that the state should shift from obscure regressive business, sales, and property taxes to income taxes. Republicans in Florida, Washington, and Colorado argued for fundamental tax reform but stressed cutting tax rates in conjunction with changing tax bases.[2]

A member of the Tennessee House Ways and Means Committee argued for tax reform as a fundamental element of an economic development policy this way:

> I offered a bill for a 4.5 percent income tax and a 4.5 percent sales tax and take [the sales tax] off food—a revenue-neutral bill, now. We could have had twenty thousand new jobs in Tennessee from what we're losing across the border in sales. . . . To give you a comparison, every $25 million we spend on infrastructure improvements provides 13,600 jobs, and here I can get you 20,000 jobs . . . by bringing people back into Tennessee to buy their groceries and some big-ticket items like a car. And I've gotten you these jobs without spending a dime on programs or tax incentives. . . . Our problem is that our tax system is inequitable, . . . and the current tax system costs us in terms of jobs here and tax reciprocity in other states.

Politicians promoting tax reform seek to change a collective good to benefit their constituents (Jackson and Hawthorne 1987). Issues of vertical transferability led legislators to view tax incidence broadly. They were concerned about the burdens imposed not just by state taxes but also by federal and local taxes. In New Jersey, Florida, and Michigan, legislators addressed issues of local property taxation in conjunction with economic development. Two New Jersey assembly members argued that the state would be at a disadvantage to contiguous states until it discontinued its reliance on local property taxes and shifted to income taxes. One of the assembly members made this argument:

> *Assembly Member:* The best thing we could do for our development is reform our property tax system and get our property taxes on a par with especially Pennsylvania but also parts of New York, Connecticut, and maybe Maryland.
>
> *GB:* How do you do that?
>
> *Assembly Member:* The best way to tax is according to affluence. . . . I don't buy into some Neanderthal notion that if you buy things you should be taxed or that we need to have a system based on two-thirds property taxes and one-third sales taxes. That's ridiculous, especially when you consider that property taxes are the most regressive taxes. The better part, too, about a stable progressive income tax is that people pay income taxes, not business, and that will encourage development.

Among legislators supporting tax incentives, a division existed between those who believed incentives genuinely created jobs and those who felt incentives were a necessary competitive response to neighboring states' policies. Among legislators whose first priority was tax incentives, only one was in the latter group, and most sincerely believed that tax incentives created jobs. Several legislators who viewed incentives as a competitive response believed that if neighboring states abandoned incentives, employers could no longer be swayed from one location to another on the basis of taxes. Consequently, states could shift their development efforts to education, infrastructure, and general tax reform.

Although the economic benefits from targeted development programs may be less dispersed than with public-goods strategies, the potential for political benefits is probably higher. Citizens who work at employers attracted by development packages may credit individual politicians with attracting commerce and industry. In addition, politicians may solicit campaign resources from employers after they locate in a particular state or district.

Several legislators viewed the competitive nature of tax incentives as a healthy component of their overall philosophy to reduce the size of government. Some legislators were so enthusiastic about offering firms tax exemptions that they promoted increasing tax rates to increase the value of the exemptions to potential employers. These legislators believed that employers would respond to tax incentives with high dollar values and found no irony between their general position that government should reduce its spending but increase its tax rates. One New Jersey assembly member argued that Governor Whitman's effort to cut tax rates made sense as a long-run strategy but that in the short run she should have raised rates so the state could offer truly valuable exemptions to current and potential employers. This assembly member correctly noted that decreasing tax rates led to a decline in the value of tax exemptions (Steuerle 1991). When I asked about this irony, the assembly member responded that rates did not matter as long as the government was exempting firms from taxes. He argued that firms would find states with monetarily valuable exemptions more attractive than those where they could not receive the same tax break. Other legislators shared the view that tax incentives should form the core of any economic development program. One Mississippi legislator indicated that he believed no tax incentive too generous, saying,

> *Legislator:* The main thing we can do for a company is offer them the tax incentives they need to come here. . . . We've been able to help some with industrial-revenue bonds, and we can help you on the AV [ad valorem tax] and give you a long payback on it to do what needs to be done.
> *GB:* Can you go too far?
> *Legislator:* No, I don't see it. Everybody says Alabama did with Mercedes, but I'd say they went all the way, and it'll pay big dividends. . . . So no, I don't think you can ever go too far because these things, incentives, follow the basic economic laws of supply and demand, and if companies demand them, we should supply them.[3]

Of the seven Democrats who gave top priority to tax incentives, four were African-American or Hispanic legislators from economically distressed areas. They felt that targeted "enterprise zone" tax incentives were critical to revitalizing their districts. Two of these four represented portions of Harlem and the Bronx in New York City. One represented a densely populated, declining section of Denver. The fourth represented several rural counties on the Mississippi Delta. These members wanted tax credits not for employers but for specific geographic locations, so that employers could benefit only by locating in a designated area. Another Colorado representative who favored focusing on education and roads funding expressed his frustration with his state's enterprise zones:

> Sure, we have enterprise zones, and those help employers, but the problem is that now over 60 percent of the state is an enterprise zone. You mean to tell me that 85 percent of Coloradans live in economically distressed areas when we have the best economic growth in the nation. The problem is that [enterprise zones] were popular, but we should have targeted them to help the 'hood' that I represent. The problem is you can't get them passed unless you can get one for the folks in Aspen, too. Now, how does that make sense? We're giving tax breaks so skiers won't be economically distressed, I guess. And we offer an employer the same benefits or better for going to Vail or Aurora instead of east Denver.[4]

Among those who indicated support for tax incentives as a second or later priority, the majority considered incentives a competitive response. In Tennessee, Mississippi, and Washington, legislators discussed their reservations about the limited efficacy of employer tax incentives. These representatives viewed incentives as somewhat influential in encouraging a plant to locate in a state but pointed out that job location differed from job creation. Nonetheless, eleven of thirteen Tennessee representatives supported the 1993 franchise tax incentives as a response to incentives in other southeastern states. Legislators discussed tax breaks offered by Kentucky in attracting Toyota, South Carolina in attracting BMW, and Alabama in attracting Mercedes.[5]

These illustrations demonstrate that the incentives for particular benefits can be substantial, and legislators may respond to them. The "tangible" political benefits from a plant opening may be worth diverting state funds or foregoing state revenues, even when doing so implies providing a lower level of public goods. Although the public-goods strategy may provide better labor markets and more equitably dispersed public benefits, representatives may find it hard to resist the competitive policies of their neighbor states and the political capital created by claiming responsibility for creating specific jobs.

After tax incentives, legislators favoring particular benefits indicated preferences for regulatory reform and reduction.[6] Specific components of regulatory changes varied from state to state, but most legislators agreed that their states needed less complex permissions processes and adjustment in fees to reflect an employer's ability to pay. Republicans generally favored reducing the number of regulations and streamlining regulatory processes. Such regulatory changes offer particular benefits to various industries. Because such regulations often help produce various public goods, such as reductions in air or noise pollution, regulatory reductions would in general increase the consumer surpluses of particular employers, their employees, and their customers at the expense of those citizens who would be less well off because of increases in various pollutions or hazards.

Few legislators indicated support for a single-prong approach to economic development. Most indicated a second priority, and some indicated as many as five priorities in their development strategies. Table 9 is a cross-tabulation of legislators' first and second priorities for economic development strategies.[7]

Table 9 indicates a partisan breakdown in economic development strategies. Among legislators who identified both their first and second economic development priorities, 40 percent of the Democrats identified education and infrastructure spending among their top choices, whereas only a single Republican (6 percent of responding Republicans) did so. Conversely, Republicans placed far more emphasis on a combination of specific tax incentives, regulatory reductions, and broad-based tax reform. Eighty-two percent of Republicans identifying multiple economic development strategies emphasized these three mechanisms. In contrast, only 32 percent of Democrats gave high priority to specific tax incentives, regulatory changes, and tax reform.

For legislators, governing is an ongoing process where policy changes are typically marginal and where one set of policies may constrain legislators from enacting their preferences in a second policy area. In the following cases these constraints prevail. Legislators find themselves constrained in their endeavors to increase the benefit/tax ratios and overall incomes of their constituents via economic development policies.

Translating Preferences into Policies: Governing Principles and Federalism

Legislators cannot simply enact their individual preferences into a series of disjoint and contradictory policies. Representatives work to create policies that enjoy majority support among their colleagues, that governors will accept, that promote specific industries, and that comport with existing tax and spending policies. In this section, I detail how legislators enacted and implemented development policies. As with the examination of tax policies in the previous chapter, the primary units of analysis are the collective decisions of the legislatures for various development programs. Also similar to the investigation of tax policies is legislators' reliance on a subset of governing principles—obscurability, dependability, equity, and vertical transferability. Competition among states, a form of horizontal transferability, provided some motivation for the development policy and shaped the alternatives legislators debated.

TABLE 9. Legislators' First and Second Priorities for Economic Development (in percentages)

Second Priority	First Priority				
	Education	Infrastructure	Tax Incentives	Regulation Reduction	Tax Reform
A: Democrats					
Education		16	8		4
Infrastructure	24				
Tax Incentives		4			
Regulation Reduction			8		16
Tax Reform	24				8
B: Republicans					
Education		6		6	
Infrastructure					6
Tax Incentives	6		6		
Regulation Reduction			19		25
Tax Reform	6		6		32

Note: For Democrats, $N = 25$; for Republicans, $N = 16$.

Before moving to the specific cases, a few general points about the policy process are in order. A state's current economic climate and conditions shape its development goals (Laver 1981; Brace 1991, 1993) While Mississippi focuses on attracting manufacturers offering wages as low as five dollars per hour as a means of raising the incomes of its relatively poor residents, New York legislators worry about losing high-wage manufacturing jobs and retaining high-paying jobs in financial services. These professions provide a substantial income tax base but also contribute to growing income inequality in the state, which concerns many assembly members. Consequently, New York legislators coupled their 1994 corporate tax reduction with the introduction of an earned-income tax credit for families making less than thirty-seven thousand dollars annually. Second, overall tax systems and constitutional requirements shape governments' economic development strategies. A state's budget constraint is a general concern for legislators and offers parameters for what policies are viable (Kingdon 1990). Constitutional provisions in Florida and Mississippi enable the state legislature to offer tax abatements from local taxes.

Legislators in Mississippi and Tennessee placed considerable emphasis on economic development. Such emphasis may not be surprising given that the two states had the lowest per capita incomes among the eleven case-study states (Lilley, DeFranco, and Diefenderfer 1993). Despite similar economic profiles, the two states have chosen very different avenues by which to pursue economic development. Tennessee has increased its spending on education and infrastructure, while Mississippi has focused on tax incentives to employers (Tennessee 1994–95). Although differences in tax structures and constitutions explain some of this divergence, politics has also shaped the policy processes in both states.

Education and Infrastructure or Tax Incentives

Tennessee and Mississippi follow divergent strategies for economic development. In Tennessee, legislators focused on increasing funding for education and infrastructure, whereas Mississippi legislators directed more of their attention to tax incentives and tax reductions. In Tennessee, all but one legislator either questioned the economic efficacy of tax incentives or suggested that incentives had bounded benefits. In Mississippi, legislators from both political parties expressed support for incentives and other particular-benefits programs.

Tennessee.   In 1993 Tennessee enacted an economic development policy that offered tax relief to new or expanding businesses by abating the state-imposed franchise tax. One of the architects of the plan explained its calculus:

> *Representative:* What knocks us out of competition . . . is the franchise tax, and that's why we now provide a break on that specific tax.
>
>   When you look at incentives, . . . you can go overboard. Alabama gave away the store with Mercedes. . . . Kentucky has a plan that's supposed to benefit depressed counties, but I don't think they've done that because they just give up the incentives, and people are fighting for those benefits. But the beneficiaries are Owensboro and Bowling Green, not the depressed counties in eastern Kentucky outside of the Georgetown-Toyota area.
>
> *GB:* So what differentiates Tennessee?
>
> *Representative:* We have a principle that we are willing to forgo a certain amount, portion, of marginal revenues. We won't forgo all revenues, and we won't go down from current revenues on a particular tax. Some states will say they absorb one incentive and a loss on a tax with a second tax, but you can never trace that. With an individual tax, you know whether you're below last year or not or how much you've given up. In our neighboring states, it's more an act of faith that the increased sales and income taxes offset franchise and property tax abatements.

Most Tennesseeans suggested that their need to respond to tax incentives from other states motivated their support for the 1993 tax incentives. Most noted that the 1993 plan followed a rule that the state would only forgo marginal future revenues. Fewer legislators admitted that constitutional and statutory provisions prevented property tax abatements and that the state's lack of gross-receipts and income taxes limited its ability to offer tax incentives paralleling those in Alabama, Kentucky, and Mississippi.

Tennessee's tax system influences its economic development in a second way. Several legislators suggested that the state's emphasis on providing infrastructure was a natural result of Tennessee's reliance on cyclical sales taxes and a historical tradition of using general revenues to pay for capital projects. Although legislators would have preferred shifting spending to education, they concluded that funding education generously one year and then cutting it dramatically the next would send a mixed signal to outside firms whose managers might expect a consistent, if not generous, education for their children. The one-time-appropriations nature of infra-structure projects with low maintenance costs relative to those of ongoing educational programs led the state to a policy whereby it invested revenue increases in flush years and cut back on these investments during recessions.

In Tennessee, representatives perceived that the benefits from education and infrastructure were more or less equally available to all citizens. Although they could not claim specific connections between tax incentives and new employers, the broader public-goods strategy appeared to have worked as Tennessee rejuvenated its economy through the 1980s by attracting two automobile assembly plants and then their component suppliers. In Mississippi, representatives could also point to attracting employers, but the benefits accrued largely to employers and even employees who worked in new plants, and facilities directly paid for some of the incentives offered to employers.

Mississippi.   Although Mississippi has a limited tax base, its policymakers have offered a variety of tax incentives. In 1993 the legislature passed a law enabling new or expanding businesses to issue industrial-revenue bonds and to offset debt service by assessing all employees between 2 and 6 percent of their salaries.[8] In turn, employees could deduct assessments from their state personal income taxes. However, because Mississippi had a relatively high personal exemption and tax rates of only 3 to 5 percent, few of the employees could recoup their assessments via income tax abatements. Because the personal-income tax credit was not refundable and could not be carried forward to future tax liabilities, the likelihood that individual employees would recoup the bond assessments to their wages decreased substantially. None of the legislators or the relevant committee staff could estimate either the costs to the state in terms of foregone income from personal income taxes or the costs to individual employees for the bond assessment fees. In addition to the debt service provided by assessments on wages, employers receive further assistance from corporate income tax credits typically equal to or exceeding the total value of assessment on wages.[9] Thus, a firm with a payroll of $2 million, paying nine dollars an hour, and owing $500,000 in debt service annually could expect a $120,000 reduction in its debt service from a 6 percent payroll assessment and approximately $154,000 in corporate tax credits. Its debt service would fall from $500,000 to $226,000 (Condiff 1993). Several textile, small-appliance, and food-processing firms have taken advantage of this credit to build or renovate plants in Mississippi.

The second tax abatement authorized by the legislature comes at the immediate expense of local governments in the form of ad valorem tax abatements. Mississippi's ad valorem taxes are property taxes imposed on items such as manufacturing equipment. A new business can attain either a reduction in its ad valorem taxes or a deferral once it agrees to locate in a specific municipality or county. Although the county can define some of the terms of the abatements, the state maintains control over their broad parameters, such as how long they last. In this way, state legislators can offer tax incentives with costs absorbed by local governments. Some legislators defended this policy, suggesting that localities would benefit from economic growth and recoup any losses from increases in the stock of taxable residential and commercial real estate. Other members took a more critical view of the abatements and suggested that only localities with a healthy tax base could afford ad valorem abatements. Consequently, only areas of the state with relatively vibrant economies could bear development costs. This development distribution further exacerbated discrepancies in local resources and further disadvantaged some localities relative to others. Nonetheless the ad valorem abatements illustrate how legislators promoted economic growth through an avenue created by vertical transferability. No similar avenue was available to legislators in Tennessee, thus partially explaining the different development strategies.

Mississippi county governments and the legislature have made wide use of ad valorem tax abatements. The generosity of these abatements was such that in 1992 the Mississippi Supreme Court ruled abatements exceeding ten years violated the state constitution. (Abatements ranged from twenty to ninety-nine years.) In response to the court's decision, the Mississippi legislature enacted a law, SB 3013, which attempted to reinstate the ad valorem abatements. In cases where county tax assessors ignored the legislature's actions and placed manufacturing property on the tax rolls, it was assessed below its market value.

One final factor discouraged several Mississippi representatives from promoting a public-goods strategy: what four representatives called the "brain drain." House members feared that spending money for education would produce a workforce whose talents would find no market in Mississippi. Educated Mississippians would leave the state after having received the benefits of its educational services. One conservative legislator cited this problem as the rationale for concentrating on bringing employers to Mississippi as opposed to training workers for jobs in a larger market-place. He stated that much funding for education was simply too nebulous for Mississippi's very specific, often low-skilled, employment needs. At one point he strongly criticized the state's effort to increase education spending, saying,

> *Representative:* Last year we passed a resolution saying we wanted to get to the Southeast average on teacher pay. Now, there is the argument that that's the way to get better people, but, meanwhile, we have to pay a lot more for current teachers who are satisfied with what they have. The second problem with it is statistical.
> *GB:* I don't understand.
> *Representative:* Well, if we raise our pay to the southeastern thirteen-state average, then that's going to raise that average, so we've got to go even higher. It's a goal we can never attain, so why start such a cycle?

Three Mississippi Democrats countered this argument by suggesting that the state needed to spend more on education and training but do so in a strategic manner. They argued that Mississippi needed to stop offering itself as the last bastion of cheap, low-skilled workers. Instead, they promoted state programs that would increase the skills of a large number of Mississippians so that the state could attract higher-wage employers. These legislators recommended focusing state resources on technical and vocational programs as opposed to offering more tax incentives or funneling money to the state universities and graduate schools.

The overall difference in strategies between Tennessee and Mississippi is striking. The differences existed in part because of basic differences in tax structure. Having no income tax, Tennessee has no opportunity to offer an assessment/credit program paralleling Mississippi's. A second reason for the differences is that Mississippi's governor enthusiastically proposed a variety of tax incentives, whereas the previous two Tennessee governors emphasized increasing funding for education and infrastructure.

Legislative leadership played a role in forming development policies in both states. In Tennessee, a chairperson of the House Ways and Means Committee enthusiastically supported Governors Lamar Alexander and Ned McWherter in their efforts to increase education and infrastructure funding. The chairperson resisted developing and presenting a tax-incentive package to the legislature and eventually did so only to placate colleagues and development officials who argued that one was necessary as a competitive response to neighboring states' policies. Once convinced, the chairperson asked a colleague who shared his skepticism to develop a tax package that would address the competitiveness issue but would not decrease the state's current revenues.

In Mississippi, the Speaker of the House enjoys the power to appoint committee chairs and has done so irrespective of party. Consequently, two Republicans who were enthusiastic supporters of tax incentives assumed committee positions that enabled them to present tax-incentive packages to the House. Both legislators proudly pointed out that once they presented an economic development package on the floor, most of their colleagues found it hard to oppose policies designed to enhance growth. Although several Democrats and a few Republicans argued that the state was underinvesting in education, they reported that they really could not garner sufficient support to defeat the development packages that had been offered in the early 1990s.

Colorado.   Like Mississippi, Colorado offered a variety of state income tax credits and local property tax deferments and abatements. However, Colorado representatives worried that a citizen-passed referendum, Amendment 1, would impede their ability to design and enact tax packages for particular employers. In 1992 the legislature failed to enact a tax-and-subsidy package designed to entice Ziff Publishing to relocate from New York and Massachusetts to Colorado. In response, the governor and legislature attempted to devise a second plan, only to find that Ziff was no longer interested in relocating. The president of the publishing firm based his lack of enthusiasm on Amendment 1, which subjects all tax measures, including development and revenue bonds, to a popular referendum vote (Leib 1993).

A bipartisan group of representatives opposed the original Ziff package, believing that the subsidies exceeded the benefits or the generosity of the package set a bad precedent for possible future tax packages. In the wake of Amendment 1, legislators suspected they could no longer design, consider, and enact tax-initiative development packages because any tax changes would be subjected to a statewide vote. Facing an antitax mood, representatives perceived that they could not wage sufficiently informative campaigns to win development-package ballots. Such campaigns would be costly in terms of both money and time and have at best uncertain, if any, political benefits.

House members concerned about Amendment 1 suspected that employers would shy away from Colorado simply because they would have to endure a relatively cumbersome and uncertain process to receive development incentives, and the experience with Ziff publishing offered preliminary evidence for this dilemma (Leib 1993).

Provisions in Amendment 1 placed Colorado at a disadvantage in attracting federal dollars. With the completion of Denver International Airport, several legislators expressed concerns that the state find jobs for those who had moved to Colorado to work on the airport's construction. One option was to transform the former Stapleton Airport into a Department of Defense finance and accounting center employing between four thousand and seven thousand people. Amendment 1 required Denver officials to place a financing plan on the ballot either to create a special tax district or to issue bonds. A Denver economic development advocate noted that the city and state were not competitive with other cities bidding for the center not because of a lack of potential facilities but because the federal officials would not have to wait for votes to locate in competing cities (Leib 1992).

General Tax Reforms and an Improved Image

Legislators in Mississippi and Tennessee liked to say that their states were open for business, and, indeed, such sentiments are consistent among both elected and administrative development officials (Eisinger 1988). In contrast, legislators in the industrial states of Michigan, New Jersey, New York, and Washington worried that complex regulations and certain tax disadvantages sent a negative message to potential employers. As with efforts to change general tax systems discussed in chapter 3, legislators responded to this dilemma symbolically.

In New York and Washington, legislators identified dependable but regressive business taxes as their primary target for development efforts. In New York, a 6 percent tax on utility receipts exacerbated the Empire State's relative disadvantage in energy costs. As the result of a budget surplus in 1994, legislators agreed to cut taxes. Despite the problems created by utility taxes, assembly members and senators targeted their tax cuts at the state's corporate profits tax and rather than at the utilities tax. An assembly member with expertise in energy taxes and their impact on utility costs explained his colleagues' decision this way:

> The best thing we could do to change the business climate is to cut our energy costs. . . . We should say, "Hey, what are the advantages and disadvantages of doing business in New York?" We have great natural resources, a relatively central demographic location . . . but we have to recognize that our energy costs are going to at best be relatively high and we need to lower them. . . .
>
> Our biggest problem with these costs is that we tax utilities. We have a gross-receipts tax on all commercially and industrially used energy, so it adds substantially to your operation costs. It makes starting a business in New York a bigger hurdle than other places would be, where not only are their energy costs lower but they don't tax them.

Several of this assembly member's colleagues agreed that as a matter of good public policy, they should address energy taxes, yet the assembly's Ways and Means Committee—and ultimately the assembly—passed a two-pronged approach to tax relief that included a reduction in the state's corporate income tax rate and the enactment of an earned-income tax credit for low-income families. Eight of the New York assembly members indicated that the mix of tax cuts resulted from a political compromise between the Democratic governor and House leadership and the Republican Senate leaders. Two of the assembly members took a somewhat cynical view of the bipartisan leadership's exclusion of the gross-receipts utility tax in favor of corporate income tax relief. One Upstate Democrat noted, "It's all image. While it would be helpful to a lot of struggling businesses with relief from utility taxes, we instead go for the headlines with a corporate tax cut—helping firms that are by definition profitable and can pay some taxes." A more conservative member suggested that the Republican leadership in the Senate had ulterior motives for concentrating on the corporate profits tax:

> The way it works in New York is that you can carry forward your [corporate] losses, so the five largest corporations in the state probably have paid no income taxes since '89. Now that means you pass a tax cut that gets a lot of attention and gives us a big probusiness image but

in fact helps very few struggling businesses and is really fairly costless. If we had gone ahead with the energy tax reductions, we really would have seen a drop in revenues—revenues we very much depend on, and the Republicans know that. This was a cheap cut that gives them the appearance of helping their big friends in business.

In Washington, a bipartisan contingent of legislators argued that overall tax reform was the optimal development policy, yet in 1994 the legislature enacted a fairly modest set of tax incentives (proposed by Governor Mike Lowery) for high-technology industries. In contrast to New York, Washington Republicans accused their Democratic counterparts of having ulterior motives. Two Republicans suggested directly that Governor Lowery's proposal was a political payoff to executives at Microsoft who had openly supported the governor in his close 1992 election. Several Democrats either corroborated this scenario or suggested one of two alternative explanations. Some contended that the tax incentives were a critical component in refurbishing a probusiness, high-technology image, while others suggested that they would have preferred comprehensive tax reform but supported the governor's proposal either out of political loyalty or because it was part of an overall tax bill that the House voted to pass en bloc.

Both Washington and New York legislators concluded that the dependability of the utility taxes in New York and the business and occupation taxes in Washington discouraged the legislature from decreasing them. Legislators also perceived that the relative obscurability of these taxes further depressed any desire to change them. They suggested that the headlines would go to the corporate tax cut in New York or to high-technology tax credits in Washington.

As in Colorado, Washington representatives faced consequences from the recent passage of Initiative 602, which limits the growth of government spending.[10] Legislators did not have to submit development proposals to statewide votes, but representatives suggested they were less likely to enact tax abatements because revenue losses could become a problem if the state's economy declined. Under the provisions of Initiative 602, any tax increases must be approved by a three-fifths majority of the House. House members felt that surmounting this hurdle made them less likely to offer tax breaks to potential employers. With the constraints imposed by Initiative 602, legislators said they would not vote to divert funds from current programs for development programs because it would be very difficult to recover funding should demand for services later change.

Conclusion: Benefits and Changes in Benefit/Tax Ratios

For representatives, deriving benefits from economic development is an uncertain enterprise, but it is one to which many legislators devoted considerable energy. With particular-benefits strategies, representatives can target resources, and such targeting may create more opportunities for claiming credit for job creation and serve as a means for mobilizing other campaign resources. Conversely, legislatures that choose to facilitate economic growth via public-goods strategies ensure that they can claim credit for government-provided education and infrastructure, if not for specific jobs in their communities. As the cases also indicate, a state's broader tax-and-spending policies, particularly for education, direct its focus toward public-goods or particular-benefits means for economic development ends.

Different economic development strategies imply different changes in citizens' benefit/tax ratios. In Mississippi's incentive-based strategies, citizens with new jobs also pay directly for those jobs by subsidizing capital formation with wage assessments. In Tennessee, citizens can receive certain benefits from increased education and infrastructure spending and have seen concomitant employment growth, for which they pay mostly through a general sales tax. Although regressive, the sales tax spreads development costs over the entire population to a larger extent than does the Mississippi tax abatement/income tax credit program. Whereas all consumers in Tennessee fund the public goods, which are then available to Tennesseeans regardless of their employment, Mississippi lowers the benefit/tax ratios of workers who gain jobs from firms locating there. Essentially, Mississippi targets the cost of its development policies at workers by allowing employers to assess debt-service costs to their employees.

New York and Washington legislators indicated strong desires to change tax policies to mitigate their states' relative development disadvantages. In both cases, political obstacles to general reforms meant that legislators settled for development policies with benefits targeted at particular firms. Other firms and businesses continued to operate under the tax policies that legislators indicated hindered development. In these states, changes in benefit/tax ratios may be minimal, and a better analysis concerns the counterfactual of the changes that could occur. If legislators in Washington and New York could pass broad-scale tax reforms, then marginally profitable firms in both states would become more profitable as their payroll and utility taxes declined. Employers could then retain higher profits, pass these benefits on to their employees in the form of higher wages, or pass benefits on to consumers by lowering prices.

The creative politics in economic development tie into the politics of taxation in the previous chapter and education finance politics in the next chapter. Many legislators consider education a critical component of their development policies. However, these legislators are concerned that the policies used to fund education are inequitable and consequently disadvantage students and school districts relative to others. They explicitly connect the payment mechanisms or taxes they impose with the public goods they fund, such as education.

Chapter 6

Education Financing: How Many Types of Equity?

The whole problem is that people pay taxes, not towns.

—Vermont representative

This lament by a frustrated Vermont representative offers an entry point into yet another avenue of politics created in a federal system. In financing education, tensions arise among state governments, localities, and citizens. On the one hand, localities want states to shoulder greater shares of financial responsibility and alleviate discrepancies in revenue capacities among localities. On the other hand, these local officials desire administrative control over their schools. Complicating these competing demands, citizens demand quality schools and property tax reform and generally resist tax increases. Court orders to equalize funding across school districts only add further complexity and add another component to intergovernmental relations.

The previous chapter examined how legislators connected education and training programs with economic development strategies. In this chapter, I consider broader issues regarding public education financing and how the provision of a public good supported by legislators links with the taxes imposed to finance it. Primary and secondary education provide the best example of a government-provided public good, and this chapter examines the variance in how states connect taxes to a public good. In the case of education, states provide thirteen years of public-school education to their citizens, so the issue is not variance in program design, as it is with tax policy, economic development, or Medicaid reform. With education, representatives struggled with three issues:

1. finding politically palatable connections between taxes and services
2. reducing the lack of responsiveness to the ability-to-pay principle created over time with the property tax, and
3. retaining the policy accountability of education.

Representatives in several states have devoted considerable attention to financing public education and to defining the appropriate role for state governments in providing public education. State responsibility for financing public primary and secondary education has grown substantially in the past two decades (Gold 1992). With respect to intergovernmental relations, education presented a situation in which the state would assume a responsibility previously held by local governments. But rather than shift resources so that localities would enjoy a windfall of revenues, most states also exercised the prerogative to constrain local tax powers. Consequently, with state assumption of education responsibility came a decrease in the revenue possibilities for localities. The state budget lines shifted out with new revenues, but so did their spending obligations. For localities, both spending and revenue contracted.

Local school districts have grown increasingly dependent on state governments for education funding and for a mechanism by which to alleviate and redress the inequities created by property taxes. The relationship between localities and state creates yet another dimension of tax politics. In this dimension, locally elected officials must reconcile three things— local control, tax equity, and the fair provision of a public good, education. How legislators navigate these politics has consequences for both state and local officials.

Education financing demonstrates that state representatives are not necessarily tax averse and will impose large new tax increases under particular conditions. The main issue vis-à-vis education revolves around vertical transferability. State legislators have been willing to increase state tax burdens to reduce inequities in local tax burdens and equitably provide a public good—primary and secondary education. In terms of distributional consequences, representatives worried that land-rich and income-rich local school districts could provide much better educations for children than could other districts and that land-rich but income-poor districts would have to impose proportionately high tax rates to maintain minimal educational standards or meet state and federal funding requirements.[1]

With property tax reform and state assumption of education financing, citizens' benefit/tax ratio changes depend on the districts in which they live and the incidence of the tax imposed as an alternative to property taxes. For some citizens, shifting from property to sales taxes will increase their benefit/tax ratios as property taxes decline more than sales tax burdens increase. For other citizens, declines in local property taxes may not offset increases in sales taxes, and benefit/tax ratios decrease. For persons renting housing, changes in benefit/tax ratios depend on whether landlords pass along property tax savings in the form of reduced rent. Another factor affecting benefit/tax ratio changes relates to interactions among state and federal tax policies. For homeowners, federal income taxes may increase as citizens lose a portion of their deduction for property taxes, which will not be offset if the state shifts to sales taxes. Several states offer "circuit breaker" programs designed to offset property tax burdens through various income tax credits and rebates. In these states, the value of property tax credits on state income tax typically decline with reductions in property tax rates or property assessments.

As with changes in income taxes, shifting from property taxes to state sales taxes creates perceptual and objective changes in benefit/tax ratios and in representatives' political-benefits calculations. In Michigan, Republicans and Democrats agreed that many residents would pay the same amount in taxes after the state mandated large property tax reductions and increased the sales tax rate from 4 to 6 percent. Despite little objective change in their tax burdens, legislators believed that constituents supported the change because of the obscurability of sales taxes relative to property taxes.

Legislators grapple with competing and contradictory demands from their constituents. Competing demands imply that different citizens want different things. Elderly homeowners want property tax relief, and parents want good schools for their children. An individual citizen's preferences may not reconcile with each other. For example, Oregon residents have demanded and voted themselves property tax relief and quality schools but have consistently refused to accept new taxes to pay for those schools.

Although conflicting and even contradictory, legislators reported similar demands for education financing across states. Citizens wanted relief from current property tax burdens and containment on future tax increases. The latitude legislators enjoyed to increase other taxes shaped the extent and content of their response to these changes. Even in New Jersey, where the politics of income tax cuts dominated property tax and education financing issues in 1993 and 1994, Republicans and Democrats recognized the potential for property tax resistance to escalate and eclipse support for state income tax cuts.

Legislators indicated a great deal of concern about equity in education, and these concerns went beyond the suburban-urban lines identified by Peterson (1981). Citizen-initiated referenda and judicially imposed education policies shape legislators' attempts to change financing for and the provision of public education. Legislators must fashion solutions for tax equity that accommodate preferences or court and constitutional mandates for service equality. In most states, courts and legislatures have interpreted service equality to mean equal spending per student. Many representatives expressed concerns that the movement away from property taxes as dedicated school revenues may lead to a decrease in policy accountability for education and a subsequent decrease in the overall political accountability of local and state governments. The accountability dynamic between state and local government changes when state governments transfer large portions of funding responsibility from localities to themselves.

Table 10 presents data from several states regarding property tax rates. The case-study states—New Jersey, Vermont, Oregon, and Michi-

TABLE 10.   Education Spending and Taxes

	Spending per Pupil	Spending per Capita	Property Taxes per Capita
New Jersey	7,315	1,030	1,268
	(2)	(5)	(3)
Vermont	5,711	965	954
	(6)	(7)	(8)
Massachusetts	5,706	805	877
	(7)	(13)	(11)
Michigan	5,073	865	950
	(13)	(8)	(9)
Oregon	4,782	822	884
	(16)	(10)	(12)
Mississippi	2,933	562	357
	(49)	(49)	(42)

Source: U.S. Department of Education 1992 for columns 1 and 2; U.S. Bureau of the Census, 1993 for column 3.

Note: Numbers in parentheses are state rankings among all fifty states and the District of Columbia.

gan—all had relatively high property taxes. They have also taken different routes in addressing these problems in recent years.

Table 10 indicates that the case-study states in which legislators debated reform measures tended to be those where education spending and property taxes were relatively high. Another way of measuring the property tax burden is as a percentage of personal income. Using this measure, Vermont imposed the heaviest burden on its citizens, with property taxes at 5.4 percent of income, followed by New Jersey at 5.15 percent, Michigan at 5.11 percent, and Oregon at 4.95 percent. This measure illustrates relative tax burdens. For the entire nation, New Hampshire imposed the heaviest property taxes, with property taxes at 6.46 percent of income, although that state has no personal-income or general sales taxes. Alabama's property tax constituted only 1.13 percent of personal income (U.S. Bureau of the Census 1993).

Legislators attempt to find a balance for education financing that preserves policy accountability for education and stabilizes or enhances the government's general political accountability. Representatives promote tax changes that their colleagues and constituents find palatable. Doing so may mean accepting an obscure funding source at the expense of tax equity or revenue dependability or compromising among these principles.

Representatives seek to apply the principle of ability to pay but differ on just what it means. For some, the income tax provides the only means by which to apply the ability-to-pay principle. For others, the sales tax suffices, with the rationale that citizens with large disposable incomes will pay more in sales taxes than will lower-income individuals. Generally, the shift from property to income taxes would better reflect citizens' ability to pay taxes vis-à-vis their gross incomes than would a shift from property to sales taxes. Given that property taxes will be traded for other taxes, higher-income citizens are thus better off when voters enact sales taxes rather than income taxes.

Legislators pursue adequate funding for all school districts. In some cases, a philosophical or ideological desire to equalize educational opportunities motivates these desires. In other cases, state constitutions, statutes, and court orders influence legislators to promote equality in education. Overlapping both these situations, some legislators supported changes because they came from districts one might describe as land rich and cash poor. In other words, as a result of holding land with high assessed values but having modest wage incomes, citizens might face onerous property taxes.

Peterson (1981) recognizes both the developmental and distributional aspects of education policy. I offer an analysis that considers these two aspects but adds new insights that were not salient a decade and a half ago.[2] The main difference is the growing perception among state representatives that property taxes are inelastic and neither responsive to nor reflective of a citizen's ability to pay. While the distributional and developmental aspects of providing education remain much as Peterson described them, I connect the politics of property taxes with providing education.

I explore efforts to grapple with education financing in Michigan, Oregon, Vermont, and New Jersey and offer corroborative information from Massachusetts and Mississippi. In the first four states, property taxes gained prominence on state agendas, but they did so with different results. Michigan legislators designed and voters enacted a $6 billion tax shift from property to sales taxes. Oregon voters enacted severe property tax limitations but failed to increase or enact alternative taxes, as Michigan did. In New Jersey, Governor James Florio's efforts to address both court-mandated funding equalization and local property tax burdens via income and sales tax increases have been rebuffed in Governor Christine Todd Whitman's efforts to reduce state income taxes. Finally, in Vermont, legislators have grappled with property tax inequities since the early 1970s and have created four programs designed to address specific distributional and funding problems created by local property taxes. By 1994 divisions existed on whether to create a fifth mechanism by which to address problems, have the state assume or redistribute all local property taxes, or raise broad-based income and sales taxes in return for reductions in property taxes. No clear consensus existed by the early spring of 1995, despite considerable efforts in the legislature and by Governor Howard Dean. Before moving to the case studies, however, I first present the problem that property taxes present legislators. I then describe legislators' preferences and their emphasis on the principles of accountability, equity, obscurability, and dependability.

Background

Since the late 1970s, states have assumed greater responsibility for financing public education, and state taxes have supplanted local taxes in many states as the primary source for school funding (Gold 1990, 1992). The basic political problems with property taxes are their lack of obscurability and their disconnection from the ability-to-pay principle. The visibility of property taxes is exacerbated by their local politics. Unlike sales and income taxes, voters in many states regularly vote to approve or disapprove various property tax ballot measures for local governments. In state after state, legislators bemoaned local property taxes and depicted them as driven by the cost of education. These representatives preferred funding education as a function of the costs in combination with tax mechanisms that reflected citizens' abilities and willingness to pay for public education. Representatives in all eleven states argued that the service being provided—education—did not solely determine the public's collective willingness or ability to pay. In addition to support for education, legislators believed that the tax mechanisms for education financing also influenced willingness to pay.

Faced with a situation in which wealthier localities can provide better education with lower property tax rates than can their less affluent neighbors, state policymakers have several options (Gramlich 1990). They may consolidate school districts and pool tax bases. Doing so evens income disparities among communities by essentially changing the parameters of the community. Consequently, all citizens in the newly formed district face the same property tax rates. A second solution is for state governments to equalize funding and tax burdens as a proportion of income across districts. Legislators may seek to equalize funding by developing matching rates for property tax revenues that favor poorer localities (Gramlich 1990). Alternatively, legislators may leave school districts to tax at whatever rates are necessary but alleviate property tax burdens by offering various state income tax rebates to ensure that citizens do not pay more than a certain proportion of their incomes in property taxes.

Legislators' Preferences and Perceptions

In approaching education financing, representatives emphasized both their individual principles and the intergovernmental and state policy parameters in which they operated. Most legislators sought to continue providing roughly equal educational benefits for the children in their states, although several Republicans suggested that benefits could be expanded and more individually tailored by moving to a system of school vouchers. On the tax side, representatives sought to reintroduce the ability-to-pay principle, which they felt was no longer applicable with property taxes. Equally important, in moving toward collective decisions, representatives in Oregon, Vermont, New Jersey, and Michigan all had to fulfill various state statutes or constitutional provisions to provide "equal" education to schoolchildren. And the states varied in their allowance for local tax prerogatives.

Education financing presents a set of contradictory pressures for state representatives. They find themselves drawn into alleviating local property tax burdens, yet doing so necessitates raising state taxes. Concomitant with changes in finance mechanisms are changes in revenue dependability and the latitude of state legislatures to raise specific taxes in the future. For example, several legislators in Michigan suggested that the increase in the sales tax was likely to be the last. Michigan's 4 percent sales tax had been low relative to neighboring states prior to 1994 and now approached the national average rate. The representatives suggested that they did not support further raising the tax or could not envision doing so.

Shifting funding responsibility from state to local governments creates potential changes in the political accountability of state and local governments and in the policy accountability associated with education. Table 11 illustrates the principles relevant to education financing and depicts the relative frequencies with which legislators mentioned the various principles.

Legislators' concerns regarding equality revolved around two issues. Many believed that the state had a responsibility to ensure, if not finance, equal educational opportunities for every child. Educational equality typically translated into providing dollars to districts based on the size of their student populations. Representatives recognized that relying on local property taxes as the primary source for education funds either limited the likelihood of equal education or proscribed it. Equal funding demands in turn implied a state solution to a local revenue problem.

The second issue with which legislators must contend when equalizing

TABLE 11. Principles in Education Financing (in percentages)

	Democrats	Republicans	Total
Equality in educational opportunity	87	48	68
Tax equity	95	48	71
Horizontal equity	67	56	62
Obscurability	38	43	40
Dependability	21	8	15
Accountability	46	22	34

Note: Total number of legislators = 51 (26 Democrats, 25 Republicans).

educational services deals less with finance policy and more with the politics of taxation and federalism. Court interventions or the threat of court decisions motivated state representatives to support alternative funding mechanisms. More political motivations came from constituents, who could vent their anger about taxes by refusing to reelect officeholders or by passing referenda limiting state and local governments' tax powers.

Tax equity concerns reigned paramount in legislators' support for adopting new state taxes to supplant local property taxes. Fifty percent of the legislators contended that the property tax was regressive and did not reflect citizens' ability to pay taxes. Such a contention runs counter to much of the literature, which assumes that property tax burdens correspond directly with income (Peterson 1981). Although the correlations between home values and property tax liabilities have been direct, they have not necessarily been proportional to citizens' ability to pay. This lack of proportionality is why legislators found property taxes regressive. Members from every case state except Tennessee suggested that the problem with property taxes is that they are taxes on commodities (houses) for which citizens can do little to change their consumption once purchases are made. Whereas with sales, excise, and even income taxes, citizens can modify their behavior in response to tax policies, their limited ability to move or challenge a property assessment leaves little recourse with respect to property taxes.

Legislators who depicted education as a "tax taker" government function provided a second way of looking at the inelasticity of the property tax. Representatives said that because citizens could not respond to property tax increases the way they could sales and income tax increases (i.e., their housing consumption was fixed, whereas their labor market behavior and "retail" consumption was not), local officials simply developed school district budgets and taxed citizens at whatever rates were required to finance the school district. Legislators contended that other government programs had to compete for whatever tax dollars were available from more volatile sales and income tax revenues and that education ought to compete among these programs.

Although many representatives indicated support for greater state responsibility for education funding, they also perceived potential pitfalls in the shift from local to state financing. Legislators voiced concerns that shifting from local funding to more general and obscure state revenues could decrease popular support for education because policy accountability would decrease. Most legislators believed that education did not suffer the political and policy accountability problems associated with Medicaid. On the contrary, representatives worried that abandoning dedicated property taxes put schools at risk of losing long-enjoyed community support. By moving from property taxes, which citizens connected to education, to a tax that flowed to general government, legislators worried that education would lose what they perceived was a safe status from citizens' antipathy toward many government programs.

A second accountability concern focused on the linkages among state and local governments. Legislators worried that the tax shift would decrease the accountability of local officials and make them less likely to try to efficiently deliver educational services. As one representative said, "How will the local residents hold [the school board members'] feet to the fire if all they have to do is send the bill to the state?" Several representatives suggested that school boards had incentives to agree to generous salary settlements with school employees who would in turn support the board members politically. The same school board members could then request the salary funds from the state government.

Transforming Preferences into Policy

Efforts to change primary and secondary education financing have met with mixed results. In Michigan, legislators offered constituents two sweeping alternatives, and voters chose a sales tax increase over an income tax increase. In other states, tax and education reforms have proceeded incrementally, with legislators tapping various revenues and altering spending formulas each legislative session. Legislators in Oregon and Massachusetts have struggled for a decade to reconcile property tax limitations, demands for equal education, and low state taxes. In Vermont, legislators find themselves at a crossroads where they must decide either to offer a sweeping transformation similar to Michigan or to continue to rework education and tax relief programs that many representatives viewed as increasingly ineffective. Finally, New Jersey assembly members found that the politics of the income tax have largely closed the door on property tax reform.

Michigan

Among the case-study states, the largest tax change occurred in Michigan, where voters enacted a $6 billion shift from property to sales taxes.

Demands for property tax reform persisted through the 1980s and early 1990s. Several political analysts credited Governor John Engler's narrow 1990 election to his pledge to reduce property taxes by 20 percent. Despite the pledge and subsequent efforts, Michigan voters defeated his first proposal for property tax reform by a substantial margin. A state senator set the stage for the changes in Proposal A in July 1993, when she added an amendment that abolished local property taxes. Governor Engler flew back to Lansing to sign the bill into law, forcing the legislature to offer a legislative alternative to the new ballot initiative. The state constitution requires that any sales tax increase be subject to voter approval but allows the legislature to change income tax rates. Consequently, the legislature devised Proposal A, under which voters could enact a sales tax increase; if they failed to do so, a statutory alternative, an income tax increase, would take effect. On March 15, 1994, Michigan voters enacted the largest single tax shift in the state's history, cutting property tax rates from an average of thirty-five mills to eight mills on primary residences and increasing the sales tax from 4 to 6 percent.

The Michigan experience indicates elected officials' willingness to increase taxes to address local tax equity problems. All of the legislators interviewed in Michigan supported abandoning the property tax as the primary funding mechanism for school finance. They differed only on which alternative should replace it. Liberal Democrats favored an income tax increase, and moderate Democrats and Republicans favored Proposal A's sales tax increase. The issue in Michigan was not whether to enact property tax relief but how to do so. The combination of the legislature's prerogative to change income taxes and the referendum process for sales tax increases afforded representatives a means by which to ensure tax reform and share responsibility for major policy changes with their constituents. Although such an arrangement might dilute some of the credit-claiming political benefits from tax reform, it also insulated representatives from the costs of possibly choosing the wrong tax alternative to local property taxes.

Table 12 outlines the elements of Proposal A as it related to individual taxpayers.

Proposal A shifted $6 billion from property taxes to sales taxes. By moving from locally retained property taxes, legislators created a mechanism by which they could increase funding for districts with relatively high property tax rates but low per-pupil spending. Implementing legislation established a spending floor of $4,200 per student. Previously, some districts in the state spent as little as $3,100.[3] At the other end of the spectrum, several districts spent more than $6,500 per pupil. In these districts, the legislature allowed the district to exceed the eight mill cap on homestead property and, with voter approval, add an additional three mills to prevent dramatic spending reductions and cuts in popular extracurricular programs.

The primary opposition to Proposal A emanated from Detroit legislators, led by the Speaker of the Michigan House of Representatives, who argued that the income tax increase was more equitable for the city's residents. They noted that the increase in the personal exemption would have benefited the city's poorest residents. Even in Detroit, various business and political leaders including Mayor Dennis Archer, executives at General Motors, and several school board members countered Detroit area representatives' opposition and publicly endorsed Proposal A. Mayor Archer cited the proposal's decrease in the state's single-business tax as a factor outweighing the regressive effects of the sales tax increase. Proposal A won narrowly in the Motor City and by a three-to-two margin in Wayne County, which includes Detroit.

Legislators cited three factors that led to the overwhelming passage of Proposal A and the concomitant rejection of the alternative income tax

TABLE 12.   Elements of Michigan's Proposal A

Proposal A	Statutory Alternative
Reduced maximum millage to 8 mills on homestead property	Maximum millage at 12 mills
Raised sales tax to 6 percent	Retained 4 percent sales tax
Lowered income tax from 4.6 percent to 4.4 percent	Raised income tax from 4.6 percent to 6.0 percent
No change in the personal exemption	Raised personal exemption from $2,100 to $3,000
Raised tobacco tax from 25 to 75 cents per pack	No change in tobacco tax
Lowered single business tax from 2.75 percent of payroll to 2.35 percent	No change in single business tax

increase. First, voters resisted an income tax increase and perceived that they would be better off with a sales tax increase and larger property tax reductions. Second, a light turnout in Detroit relative to that for previous ballot initiatives may have helped swell the margin of victory. Third, the advertising campaign against Proposal A backfired when supporters revealed that tobacco companies ran misleading advertisements in an effort to derail the fifty-cent-per-pack tobacco tax included in the package.

Polls prior to Proposal A's passage indicated strong and growing support for the measure. Table 13 illustrates that support for the ballot initiative grew during the campaign and apparently climaxed with the actual vote, when 71 percent of those voting supported the sales tax changes over the income tax increase.

The obscurability of the sales tax made it marginally appealing. Supporters and opponents suggested that citizens simply resisted the sales tax less, and several Democrats noted that they supported the measure because the sales tax encountered less opposition among their constituents than did the income tax. Senior and junior members recalled how the previous income tax increase, enacted in the depths of the 1983 recession, had led to the recall of two legislators and a movement to recall Governor James Blanchard.

The tobacco industry provided a second component in the victory for Proposal A. In the closing weeks of the campaign, newspapers reported that out-of-state tobacco companies financed advertisements against Proposal A that depicted continuing property taxes and increased sales and income taxes. Governor Engler seized on these ads in his campaign speeches and wrote in an editorial,

There will be an aggressive ad campaign, bankrolled by the tobacco industry, to confuse voters. The tobacco lobby and its allies are only

TABLE 13. Support for Proposal A

Date	Favor	Oppose	Undecided
January 9, 1994 (poll)	50	26	24
February 13, 1994 (poll)	60	20	20
March 15, 1994 (vote)	71	29	

Source: Poll conducted by EPIC/MRA, Lansing, Michigan, on interviews with 600 likely voters. Polls have error margins of 4 percent.

concerned about their profits, not about Michigan schools and the way they are funded.

They don't like the fact that Proposal A raises the tax on a pack of cigarettes by 50 cents. They apparently don't want you to know what the state Department of Public Health knows: Michigan would be a healthier state if Proposal A passes. It is estimated that with Proposal A there could be 100,000 fewer smokers and 48,000 lives saved. (Engler 1994)

Campaign analysts, pollsters, and community activists agreed that the $3 million media opposition campaign funded predominantly by tobacco companies backfired in the final days before the vote and increased support for the proposal among moderate voters (Hornbeck and Cain 1994; Holyfield 1994). Calls for tax reform spanned the state's ideological spectrum. Legislators cited the Kalkaska crisis as the motivation from which Republicans and Democrats came to see property tax reform as inevitable. At that point, the state income tax circuit breakers no longer mattered if schools could not operate. After the election, Governor Engler stated, "We were approaching an educational meltdown, and it was the root of inequities in per pupil spending among districts" (Celis 1994).

With Proposal A's enactment, the Michigan state government's share of education funding swelled from 33 percent in 1993 to 79 percent in 1995. In Oregon, a similar shift has transpired, but legislators there have had to contend with consistent citizen rejections of sales tax proposals.

Oregon

Although Michigan's experience with property tax reform is fairly recent, Oregon's odyssey, which began in 1990, offers insights into the consequences of requiring lower property taxes. In 1990 Oregon voters enacted Measure 5, which mandated substantial property tax reductions. At approximately the same time, a court interpretation of the state constitution's provision that the state "provide a uniform system of public schools" for its citizens led to a situation in which the state legislature had to reconcile competing demands to provide more funding and to equalize funding on a per-pupil basis among school districts. The need for greater aggregate funding arose because localities would simply have fewer property tax revenues with which to finance education. Five years after the enactment of Measure 5, and despite budgets designed to equalize funding, Oregon legislators suggested that the system still needed change.

Like Michigan, Oregon's share of primary and secondary education funding rose from 28 percent in 1989 to 69 percent in 1995. Unlike Michigan, where the legislature offered a popular referendum that guaranteed alternative funding to school property taxes, Oregon voters mandated property tax relief with no alternative tax. Because of constitutional provisions, the legislature can change only income tax rates; it cannot institute a new tax. Establishing a sales tax requires voter approval, which presents a situation identical to that of Michigan. Thus, voters in Michigan agreed to raise an existing tax to provide property tax relief. Voters in Oregon have consistently rejected the creation of a new tax but have nonetheless demanded property tax relief.

Oregon representatives find themselves searching for resources in ongoing efforts to meet the conflicting demands of their state constitution, citizen support for quality education, and the voter-enacted Measure 5.[4] Republicans and Democrats alike described the budget process in Oregon as one of "backfilling" budgets with money transferred from state lottery funds to meet commitments to education and fund other general programs.[5] Measure 5 required property tax reductions for school revenues over five years: the maximum rate of fifteen dollars per thousand dollars of assessed value dropped to five dollars per thousand dollars of assessed value by July 1995. Table 14 presents the scheduled rate reductions.

With a constitutional mandate to provide equal funding for students and a voter-imposed referendum mandating property tax reductions, Oregon representatives have responded with a three-pronged strategy. First, they have repeatedly delayed the target date for reaching equalized fund-

TABLE 14.   Measure 5—Oregon Property Tax Reductions

Fiscal Year	School Taxes	Nonschool Taxes	Total Property Tax
1991–92	$15.00	$10.00	$25.00
1992–93	$12.50	$10.00	$22.50
1993–94	$10.00	$10.00	$20.00
1994–95	$7.50	$10.00	$17.50
1995–96	$5.00	$10.00	$15.00

Source: Oregon Legislative Revenue Office, 1995b.
Note: Rates are per $1,000 of assessed property value.

ing and argued to state courts that as long as they progress toward equalization, court intervention is not necessary. Second, legislators have twice canceled state income tax rebates and transferred them to education funding. Legislators argued that they did not violate Oregon's state spending limits, which trigger tax rebates, by defining the suspension of income tax rebates as property tax relief rather than as education spending. Finally, the legislature has shifted resources from other departments, particularly human services, to continue to progress toward equalizing education funding across school districts.

In the 1995 House session, increased Republican strength appeared to close the option of retaining the income tax rebates, or "kickers." A group of House Republicans informed their leadership that they would oppose any effort to withhold the kickers. By the middle of the session, it appeared that the kickers would be distributed as part of a compromise on both education spending and tax policy.

Faced with a mounting challenge to replace school funding lost via property tax reductions, the legislature voted to offer a ballot initiative to enact a state sales tax.[6] In 1993 Measure 1 created a 5 percent sales tax, provided an earned-income tax credit and sales tax credit for Oregon's income tax, raised the state's corporate-profits tax, and accelerated the elimination of all school property taxes. In November 1993 voters rejected Measure 1 by a three-to-one margin, leaving legislators with the conundrum of replacing lost local school property taxes with increasingly limited state resources.

Legislators proposed several reasons why Measure 1 failed. Many suggested that opposition to sales taxes was in some sense unique to Oregon: "It's part of being an Oregonian to oppose the sales tax" was a typical comment from both Democrats and Republicans. A second reason for the measure's failure was that it contained numerous and complicated exemptions that voters perceived as creating special tax breaks for selected interest groups, and opponents publicized these exemptions during the campaign. Finally, legislators noted that unlike Michigan, where the trade between sales and property taxes was tangential to property tax reductions immediately following the sales tax increase, Oregon's Measure 1 merely accelerated property tax reductions mandated by Measure 5. As one legislator analyzed the situation, "All Measure 1 did this last time was speed up what citizens had already voted themselves, and in the end they're left with another damned tax. They'd rather stick with the devil they've come to know in Measure 5."

Several representatives suggested that the best chance they had to convince voters to enact a sales tax had been in the late 1980s, when voters considered Measure 5. At that time, the legislature proffered a sales tax referendum that nearly passed, receiving 47 percent of the vote. One legislator suggested that the undoing of that proposal came when opponents publicized a line at the bottom of the initiative that read, "The legislature reserves the right to change the sales tax rate at any time." Legislative supporters agreed that by disconnecting the sales tax from education funding and property tax replacement, they had reduced the probability of ever mounting a successful campaign to enact a sales tax. Several legislators suggested that this realization had led to a lackluster effort on behalf of Measure 1. For example, the measure won approval to be placed on the ballot by a razor-thin vote of thirty-one to twenty-nine in the House of Representatives.

Without the sales tax and with continuing reductions in property taxes, Republicans and Democrats predicted that other programs would suffer as Measure 5 became fully effective. The Legislative Revenue Office estimated that to comply with Measure 5 the legislature would have to cut slightly more than $1 billion from an annual $6.5 billion budget (Oregon Legislative Revenue Office 1995a). Even with the sales tax, noneducation spending would have been $400 million less than the amount needed to fund programs at their level when the property tax reductions began in 1991. This figure represents about a 6 percent decrease in services.

In the aftermath of Measure 5, Republicans, Democrats, and education lobbyists agreed that one of the ironies of the measure was that the benefits did not flow to middle-income home owners. Measure 5 called for all property to be assessed at full market value. These new assessments reduced the benefits from rate reductions as individuals found that their assessment increases offset any rate decreases. Five years following Measure 5's enactment, the organization representing school administrators issued reports documenting that a majority of benefits from Measure 5 flowed to commercial real estate owners in Portland, where assessments had been close to market value in 1990. Consequently, those with large assessments in Portland suffered little from reassessment in 1990 and benefited greatly from annual rate reductions. Overall property tax rates fell from 2.7 percent of assessed value in 1989 to 1.8 percent by 1994, but these reductions fell unevenly. In some rural counties, the tax limits forced a reduction amounting to more than 10 percent of the previous year's revenues. In other counties, updating assessments to full market value actually led to effective tax increases, as rate decreases were more than offset by assessment increases (Oregon Legislative Revenue Office 1995a, C-3).

In Oregon, contradictory measures severely constrain legislators' tax options. Measures propounding sales taxes have failed consistently, and representatives saw little likelihood that such an initiative would pass or even that an increasingly conservative legislature would again place it on the ballot. Thus, legislators hope that a combination of population and income growth will allow the state to eventually reach its equalized funding goals without having to raise the income tax or dramatically cut other programs. One legislator described the situation as follows: "It's ironic that we rely on the lottery to backfill our education budget, because we're gambling that we can fund things in Oregon. . . . As long as the economy grows, we're okay, but if it slips, we have to hope people play a lot of video poker to fund our schools." Massachusetts's experience indicates that when economic growth falters, the ramifications of property tax limitations become magnified and complicate the policy process at a time when states can ill afford new initiatives.

Massachusetts

Massachusetts's experience with property tax limitations has been similar to Oregon's with the notable difference that Massachusetts voters enacted Proposition 2½ fifteen years prior to Oregon's Measure 5. With the passage of time, Massachusetts legislators have coped with the unenviable task of contending with a tax limitation during the recession that gripped the Bay State from the late 1980s through the early 1990s.

Proposition 2½ has resulted in demands from local officials for increased school funding to alleviate the discrepancies between wealthy and low-income districts. As in Oregon, legislators contended with the threat of court intervention as the gaps among localities grew over time. In response to both demands from local school officials and the threat of court-mandated equalized funding, the legislature passed and Governor William Weld approved an education-reform package in 1993.

One question that arose was why education reform had become prominent nearly a decade and a half after the enactment of Proposition 2½. Most legislators agreed that growing revenues in the 1980s and an expanding housing stock delayed the negative fiscal effects from Proposition 2½ until the state slid into recession in the late 1980s. Four Democrats noted that they had no money to redistribute in the early 1990s and were glad the litigation regarding school financing moved slowly through the courts. As the state's economy began to recover in 1993, the legislature and governor agreed to begin funneling additional revenues into education in an effort to hold any litigation in abeyance. Again an exogenous force, the power of the courts, creates a different politics for state representatives than would otherwise be the case.

Despite education-financing reforms, every legislator I interviewed expressed concerns that once the state had used various one-time revenues to pay for education reform it would no longer be able to fund the program. This situation led to a movement to enact a graduated income tax in Massachusetts. Several Democrats and some Republicans had endorsed a "grad tax" proposal to fund the education-reform act. None of the individuals I interviewed believed it would pass in the current legislature or even be seriously debated. One Republican supporter stated flatly that Governor Weld had indicated he would veto the measure and that there was no sense in expending considerable energy passing legislation that would fail at the governor's desk. Even without the governor's opposition, few legislators appeared optimistic that the bill would pass. They cited citizen distrust of government and disdain for the income tax as the principal obstacles.

Three of the eight legislators interviewed suggested that the state would be better off increasing the sales tax from 5 to 6 percent. All three suggested that the relative obscurability of the sales tax coupled with its simplicity relative to changing income and property taxes would generate greater citizen support for a sales tax solution to property tax problems.

Vermont

Vermont representatives debated tax reforms in both the 1993 and 1995 sessions but did so with little hope of enacting broad reforms. Whereas Michigan legislators agreed that the time had come to abandon property taxes for a higher income or sales tax, no such consensus had yet emerged in the Green Mountain State, resulting in considerable political confusion and posturing. Liberal Democrats divided between those who favored state control of the property tax and those who favored increasing income or sales taxes to alleviate local property taxes.

Among moderates a variety of schemes gained support, including various "tax sharing" proposals, in which property tax rates would be equalized across localities and wealthy localities would remit a portion of their revenues to the state. Vermont would in turn transfer these revenues to less prosperous localities. A second group of moderates favored increasing funding for the state's four tax equity programs, all of which had only part of the funding required for them to be fully effective.

Conservatives favored a combination of increased funding for tax equity programs and requirements for schools to lower their costs.[7] No Republican favored state assumption of the property tax, although some said they would support a statewide teachers' contract as a means of controlling salary costs. Most Republicans fell into one of three groups. The first group favored initiating a system in which the state government received a portion of property tax revenues from wealthier localities and remitted this money to poorer localities. The second group favored greater funding of the four state property tax equity programs. The third and most conservative group favored reducing the state's financial role in an effort to encourage localities to control their costs. Supporters of this strategy hoped to signal local officials that the state would no longer fund locally negotiated teacher salary settlements.

In early 1995 the House sent a measure, H. 351, to the Senate. The bill would have created a system of property tax sharing whereby wealthier communities would have remitted a portion of their property taxes to the state, which in turn would disperse the money to localities with smaller tax bases. The measure enjoyed bipartisan support among House moderates, with seventeen members cosponsoring the bill. One Republican proponent ventured that the hostile opposition from both sides assumed that a solution could be enacted in a single piece of legislation. This representative argued that once the principle of tax sharing became law, it would be easier to incrementally reconfigure tax and allocation formulas, which had been the subject of heated debate. He further elaborated how some of his more conservative colleagues had said they opposed the bill because it called for fifty wealthier towns to remit taxes to the state. These Republicans said they thought only seventeen towns should contribute. Nonetheless, the bipartisan group offered H. 351 to begin the process of property tax reform using a continuation of the sales tax and a reconfiguration of property taxes and avoiding the income tax. One legislator in this group reflected the position of his Democratic colleagues:

> Personally, I think we need to finance schools according to a citizen's ability to pay, and that means income taxes. The problem is that we already are in the income tax trough pretty deep.
>
> Now we're back to trying to fund rebates. Well, that's been going

on for fifteen years, and it's not working because people are dissatisfied with their taxes, and the discrepancies in school funds are growing. But we also have no cohesiveness on [tax] policy. We're going to lower the sales tax, which is a $30 million loss. It's an astonishing paradox that we're cutting state taxes when we need to pool our resources to help people on the property tax they deplore. And tourists would help with a higher sales tax.

Moderate Democrats and Republicans promoted incremental property tax reform lest they find themselves repeating the health-care debacle that occurred during the previous session. H. 351 introduced the concept of "equalized yields" and sharing property taxes among localities. One Republican in this group explained the strategy:

What people in the chamber have to realize is that 351 is not a solution. It's the first step that creates the principle that towns need to share their resources, and it stops us from pitting town against town. For my colleagues in the Republican caucus to oppose this simply as a local-control issue is ludicrous because we have to realize that a lot of liberals live in the gold towns and hate us, and a lot of farmers making twenty grand a year and paying six of it in property taxes still form our constituency, but they're not going to vote for anybody if they lose their farm.

Despite the passage of H. 351 in the House, the Senate refused to vote it out of committee. Some House Democrats who supported the measure suggested that they would oppose any further compromise that did not include the income tax. No Republican I interviewed supported this plan, and several indicated that they would oppose income tax increases. One of the Democrats opposed to H. 351 explained its limitations:

I'm against the so-called bipartisan compromise in 351 because it only puts horizontal equity on the table. In other words, we can't just make towns equal because you have rich people in poor towns and poor people in rich towns, and we need to get them to pay according to their ability to pay.

Unlike Michigan, where legislators saw political advantages to offering tax options to their constituents, or Oregon, where legislators had tax changes imposed on them by voters, Vermont does not have a referendum process. Most representatives recognized that this situation placed the burden for property tax reform squarely on the legislature and governor. Some found this advantageous, although most noted they could suffer the political fallout from the continuing tensions created by local property taxes and divided state government. Nonetheless, every legislator except one insisted that the legislature and governor would continue to seek compromises and solutions to the property tax problem into the foreseeable future.

Mississippi

Vermont's experience with taxes and education is in many ways similar to Mississippi officeholders' efforts to increase education funding via a 1992 sales tax increase. Legislators recognize that not all localities are capable of providing equal services when they rely on property taxes. Coincidentally, politics dictated that legislators could not increase income taxes even when they believed the services provided should be financed according to citizens' abilities to pay. The resulting compromises in Mississippi and Vermont have been bipartisan agreements to have the state shoulder more responsibility for education financing but to do so with sales taxes. In Mississippi, the legislature raised the sales tax from 6 to 7 percent, and Vermont delayed a one cent decrease in the sales tax rate and thus retained its 5 percent rate. In both states, principal proponents of the spending proposals indicated their preferences for income taxes as applications of the ability-to-pay principle. However, building the necessary support for these proposals necessitated compromising on the tax mechanism. Although Mississippi legislators increased sales taxes and Vermont legislators eliminated a sales tax cut, they did so in efforts to alleviate other tax inequities. State representatives contend with pressures not to compound federal income taxes, to treat localities fairly in providing services, and to raise revenue in the least politically objectionable manner.

Although both Mississippi and Vermont shifted to a greater reliance on sales taxes for education financing, there were substantial distributional differences for the citizens in each state. In Vermont, the delay of the sales tax cut implied only that citizens would not benefit from lower taxes and that no one would face a higher tax burden than already existed. In Mississippi, the rate increase would affect any citizen who made purchases. Moreover, Mississippi does not exempt food from its sales tax, and, consequently, its tax shift was more regressive than Vermont's. Furthermore, Vermont's delay of the sales tax decrease enabled it to fund programs designed to address and alleviate the regressivity of its local property tax burdens.[8]

New Jersey

In Vermont, Michigan, and Oregon, education-finance reform proceeded in those states' larger political and tax contexts. In New Jersey, the opposite has transpired. The politics of the income tax have stalled efforts to alleviate political and local problems created by property taxes. Politicians in both parties agreed that pursuing income tax reductions would encourage demands for property tax reforms but differed on the shape those reforms would take given the rejection of Governor Florio's addition of a progressive income tax in 1990 and Governor Whitman's commitment to reducing income taxes.

In the previous case studies, I have offered examples of states assuming greater responsibility for local schooling or debating how to do so. In New Jersey, the movement to cut state taxes offers further evidence regarding legislators' concerns for both overall (i.e., state and local) tax equity and service provision. Republicans and Democrats expressed concerns that Governor Whitman's tax proposals would lead to greater inequities in the state's already relatively high tax burdens. Nonetheless, Democrats saw little possibility of changing the course of taxes, and Republicans believed that for political reasons, they had no choice but to cut the income tax. Several Republicans noted the need for property tax reform but felt they could neither relent on their pledge to cut income taxes by 30 percent nor raise the sales tax. One senior Republican suggested legislation that would have introduced state-provided financial incentives to localities in return for keeping their property tax rates low. He explained,

> I've sponsored legislation that would check local and county school districts. It would indicate the property tax could not be raised more than the CPI [consumer price index] plus 1 percent. It's time school districts stopped buying their labor peace by these huge 6, 7, and 8 percent salary settlements. . . . The property tax incentive act would mean that if a community could maintain or reduce its property tax load, we would offer them additional state aid. And even in this year's budget I can find $14 million as an incentive to do that.

Facing simultaneous demands for lower property and income taxes, this legislator offered a compromise that would set New Jersey on a path similar to those in Vermont, Oregon, and Michigan—correcting inequities in the property tax with credits and reductions in the income tax. If other states' experiences are any indication, these remedies eventually become inadequate or ineffective, and they often generate unintended consequences. At best, these remedies postpone dealing with discrepancies among localities created by property taxes. In the case of this legislation, several opponents argued that only wealthy school districts with low tax rates and slack in their budgets would be able to meet the spending targets and draw down additional state aid, which could be used to lower property tax rates even further.

Several Democrats and two Republicans suggested that if calls for property tax relief became so loud that the assembly could neither ignore them nor blame localities for profligate local spending, raising the sales tax would be the best means of redress. Although no Republican seriously suggested doing so, several observed that raising the sales tax would provide more state money and allow Governor Whitman to keep her commitment to reduce income taxes. Nonetheless, several Republican leaders suggested two reasons for not doing so.

New Jersey's education finance has been under continual court review. Assembly members suggested that they would resist any tax changes as long as the courts found their progress toward education equality adequate. In the event that this progress slowed, however, the court could impose a funding solution necessitating a tax increase, and assembly members indicated that they wanted to retain the current 1 percent "slack" in the sales tax for just such a court order. As one assembly member said, "Most people just don't mind the sales tax. I've had constituents come up to me and say, 'Hey why don't you go ahead and put the penny back on the sales tax?'"[9]

The second reason had partisan political overtones. The Republicans wanted to resist any and all state tax increases to avoid giving Democrats the ability to claim that Republicans cut the progressive income tax for wealthy citizens and raised the regressive sales tax for poor citizens. One Republican explained the situation:

Assembly Member: I have to tell you I see no better alternative to the property tax. It's a very punitive and regressive tax, so certainly the state doesn't want to assume responsibility for it in some redistribution plan. But we've had to commit to reducing the income tax—the Republican majority has made that a priority. And if we went to raise the sales tax, the Democrats would scream that that's regressive, so we won't be doing that out of deference—or pragmatism, I guess, is more like it.

GB: Do you mean deference to the Democrats?

Assembly Member: Yes, well, I mean, we're not going to give them that weapon—it's not really deference—more like defense.

Other Republicans noted that the party's strategy had been calculated beginning with the 1991 midterm election, when the Republicans gained a two-thirds majority in both chambers of the legislature in the wake of Governor Florio's 1990 tax increase on both income and sales taxes.[10] Facing a veto-proof legislature, Governor Florio agreed to rescind the 1 percent increase in the sales tax rate in 1992 but left his income tax intact. Subsequently, Whitman campaigned against the governor's income tax increase during the 1993 campaign, and she won narrowly. Having captured the governorship and retaining majority control of both houses, the Republicans perceived their tax strategy to have worked and were reluctant to give Democrats the same campaign opportunity.

New Jersey illustrates how politics overlap in federal systems. Governor Whitman has campaigned for income tax reductions as a progrowth measure, yet local officials worry that any developmental benefits will be offset if they must increase local property taxes to meet the state's basic education standards. For some localities, the state tax changes and losses of state aid to education imply that they will be at a disadvantage in the limited politics of local government. For other localities, the loss of state assistance and pressure to raise property taxes may be offset by the benefits accruing to high-income individuals who will gain from a 30 percent reduction in their state income tax liabilities.

Discussion

The education studies produce four points. First, current taxes and tax rates influence the extent and content of legislative proposals for local property tax reform. Second, the mechanisms for changing taxes—legislative, judicial, and popular referenda—influence both proposals and collective decisions. Third, the current politics surrounding education may influence both the willingness of legislators to respond at all to calls for property tax relief and the extent of those responses. Fourth, many Republicans and a few Democrats who saw a need to address property tax inequities also believed a state solution implied that they introduce some mechanism by which to control local education costs, particularly salaries.

One Oregon legislator elaborated on the need for greater state control of locally administered education, given the increased role of state funding:

> On K–12 I think what's going to happen is that we have to move to a statewide salary schedule. . . . There is a perception right now that the unions have a stranglehold on communities, and that's unacceptable. . . . What's happened with teachers is that their settlements are compared across districts, but they're out of line with what's happening in the economy generally. If you look at personal income, Oregon is 10 percent behind the nation, but we're fourth in terms of what we pay teachers.

Legislators find themselves dealing with contradictory demands. Several Oregon legislators noted that they supported property tax relief and opposed a sales tax because not doing so would jeopardize their careers. At the same time, they admitted the difficulty of trying to govern when citizens demanded relief and the courts demanded equal schooling. These political pressures complicate the tasks elected officials face as they attempt to provide goods and services for their constituents.

The mechanisms for policy change—both within and outside legislative institutions—affected policy proposals and collective decisions. In Michigan, the legislature devised a scheme that ensured reform—indeed, necessitated it—and voters expressed their preferences for sales taxes over income taxes in overwhelming numbers. Oregon legislators continue to rely on economic growth and lottery revenues to satisfy demands for funding equalization without being able to impose new taxes, and they continued to respond to the confluence of popularly passed referenda that interacted to constrain both resources and policy choices. Underlying the referenda effects were court interventions monitoring Oregon's progress in achieving equal funding. In Vermont, divided control of the legislature has led to a situation in which legislators and the governor first compromised and agreed to a sales tax cut instead of an income tax cut and then postponed the sales tax rate reduction to meet demands for property tax relief.

Current political and economic conditions shaped representatives' willingness to address equity issues across localities created by school taxes. In New Jersey, the 30 percent income tax reduction necessitated that localities grapple with their own property tax situations. In the short term, it implied that some localities—those with relatively ample resources and low tax rates—would gain an advantage over other localities in pursuing development objectives.

In Michigan, Detroit politicians supported Proposal A in part because it lowered business and property taxes, although it raised the sales tax. In Vermont, legislators debated whether to raise taxes on towns that had benefited from growing tourism to help towns with more modest resources. Some legislators argued that doing so would cripple the state's economy, while others contended that it was the only way to provide education. Vermont representatives ultimately decided to use marginal sales tax revenues from a growing economy to address inequities in tax burdens and local school spending created by local school property taxes. In both Michigan and Vermont, the issues for local officials began with the willingness of the state to address education financing—an issue related to both development and distribution.

The question left open by school-finance reform was how it would change the long-term policy accountability of public education and the overall political accountability of state and local governments. Representatives in every state voiced concerns about a "disconnect" created by shifting financial responsibility from localities to states while retaining local administrative responsibility. In another vein, representatives worried that no longer dedicating property taxes to schools would decrease public support for schools as their funding became another line in state general funds subject to political and economic fluctuations for support.

In this chapter I have focused on the politics between states and localities. The political challenges for legislators were to find a less objectionable but still revenue-sufficient tax, to create greater equity in financing across school districts, and to retain or enhance the policy accountability of public education. Overall, representatives sought to defuse impending political and financial crises by finding a palatable tax for a relatively popular public good—primary and secondary education. In the next chapter, I examine federal-state relations by investigating how Medicaid spending has affected state legislators' views on a government redistribution program designed to benefit low-income citizens and how the avenue of federalism relevant to the program, federal matching grants, has shaped both the development of the political problems surrounding Medicaid and the reforms legislators debate.

Whereas problems with education financing revolved around taxes and local control shifting to state responsibility, state Medicaid crises have been driven by spending and by federal mandates to increase coverage and services. Whereas the political challenge with education was to find a tax that sustained public support for education, the challenge with Medicaid was to control costs and generate obscure revenues to abate public resentment for an unpopular benefits program.

Chapter 7

Health Care—Afflicted Budgets

While Congress and the Clinton administration spent much of 1994 debating and ultimately failing to enact health-care reform, several state legislatures succeeded in enacting health-care reforms. In other states, the results were similar to those at the federal level—the legislature failed to effect changes despite considerable efforts (Pear 1994a). I examine health-care reform efforts in 1994–95 in Oregon, Vermont, Tennessee, Florida, Washington, and Colorado. Tennessee, Oregon, and Washington revised their states' Medicaid programs or offered health-insurance subsidies to low-income individuals. In Colorado, legislators and the governor retreated from a plan to replace Medicaid with an expanded managed-care program. Florida and Vermont representatives failed to enact health-care reforms designed to control Medicaid costs and expand insurance coverage.

With Medicaid, legislators found themselves facing high political costs for a particular-benefits program. Because of continual cost increases, state representatives faced either raising taxes or cutting services to continue providing benefits and attracting federal matching grants. This problem was compounded because Medicaid benefits for those under age sixty-five were often conditioned on the household head being unemployed, a situation many legislators found inequitable and perceived created resentment for public-health programs among constituents.

This chapter makes three contributions to the understanding of legislators' efforts to maximize benefit/tax ratios and how governing principles shape these efforts. First, legislators began to transform Medicaid from a redistributive program, offering particular benefits, to a program more closely resembling a public good, offering subsidized benefits to a broader group of citizens. Lawmakers did so not because they preferred public goods to particular benefits but because of the inequities created by Medicaid and the concentration of benefits to unemployed low-income families while the working poor were typically ineligible. Legislators referred to their concerns about citizens' abilities to pay for health care and about whether citizens deserved to pay for and benefit from public-health programs. After thirty years of rising costs, state officials favored changes because Medicaid created constant financial stress and because it had lost political support. In terms of governing principles, legislators could not ask citizens for annual tax increases for Medicaid because the program lacked policy accountability. This lack of policy accountability forced legislators to cut spending in other areas, which in turn threatened state governments' overall political accountability.

Representatives supported incorporating managed care into Medicaid because doing so created alternatives to address the inequities created by offering Medicaid to the unemployed but not to low-income workers and their families. Managed-care alternatives offered a means to apply both the ability-to-pay and deserves-to-pay principles. With the introduction of co-payments, beneficiaries would to some extent pay when they used health services and thus deserved to pay. Proposals for sliding-scale premium subsidies in Tennessee, Oregon, Vermont, and Florida reflect an application of the ability-to-pay principle.

Health politics' second contribution to the understanding of subnational politics and changes in benefit/tax ratios is that federal policies and politics influenced the parameters of state policies and politics. When introduced in 1965, Medicaid created state matching grants to establish programs and provide benefits. Forty-nine states accepted the federal government's bargain in 1965, and Arizona later enacted a modified program. At the outset, program costs were relatively modest. The replacement of the federal-state Kerr-Mills medical assistance program with Medicare for the elderly had left states with slack resources with which to fund Medicaid (Pauly and Granneman 1983). But by accepting this federal matching-grant program, the states unwittingly set the stage for their own health-reform politics in the 1990s.

The grant structure of Medicaid and waivers from the Health Care Financing Administration influenced the shape and success of state reforms. For example, concerns about vertical transferability emerged as legislators tried to retool Medicaid while retaining federal matching grants. Consequently, state representatives designed reforms and negotiated federal waivers in which they would be "held harmless" should they succeed in generating Medicaid savings. Representatives worked to ensure that savings from reform would flow to newly insured citizens and to state general-revenue funds.

National politics flowed into health-reform efforts in Colorado, Washington, and Florida. As with income tax politics, federal politics directly and indirectly influenced state health-care politics. In every case-study state, legislators related how the Clinton administration's proposals and reactions from nationally prominent Republicans shaped specific proposals and the political climate for health-care reform.

The third contribution to the understanding of benefit/tax ratio changes is that tax options available to legislators shaped both stopgap Medicaid changes and long-term reform efforts. Obscurability and equity considerations led legislators to promote sin taxes as the primary means of financing reform.[1] Subsequently, these very narrow tax bases restricted the expansion of Medicaid/managed-care coverage. Constituents' willingness to accept and legislators' willingness to vote for such taxes were components in reform measures in all the case-study states. For legislators, sin taxes presented justifiable funding because representatives could explain to constituents that citizens who put their health at risk by smoking or drinking alcohol deserved to pay for public-health programs. Lawmakers also believed that their constituents would be less likely to revolt against sin taxes than against sales or income tax increases. These financing strategies provide evidence that representatives explicitly link taxes to the services they provide.

Representatives sought benefits for a variety of constituencies. All legislators sought to control rising Medicaid costs, achieve greater health-insurance coverage, and subsequently offer tax cuts or spending increases in education, anticrime, and transportation programs. Yet the initial focus was on Medicaid funding crises. Legislators sought to alter the Medicaid program because it offered particular benefits with alarming cost increases to people whom many citizens and legislators viewed as undeserving or no more deserving than low-income workers. As outlined in chapter 2, if costs are visible and burdensome and representatives perceive a program to be politically unpopular, then a program may be unsustainable. This was the situation with Medicaid. In response, legislators sought to transform a particular-benefits program into broader managed-care programs.

Liberal legislators emphasized increasing both the economic and physical well-being of Medicaid beneficiaries and the working poor who lacked health insurance. Representatives promoted ongoing doctor-patient relationships and incentives for preventive care. For Medicaid beneficiaries, legislators sought increased health benefits and an end to the "welfare stigma" associated with Medicaid. For the working poor, representatives wanted to eliminate the inequity of entitling unemployed single parents to Medicaid but denying benefits to working individuals and their families.

Moderate and conservative legislators emphasized the fiscal benefits of controlling Medicaid costs. These representatives argued that taxpayers would benefit if more persons enrolled in health-insurance plans and thus decreased the amount of uncompensated care provided. With the decrease in uncompensated care, legislators forecast decreases in the practice of shifting the costs of uncompensated care onto private, insured (and therefore paying) patients. The fiscal slack resulting from decreases in Medicaid appropriations could in turn finance tax reductions or increased spending.[2] These legislators stressed correcting the inequities of Medicaid and offering health insurance to the working poor, explaining that such individuals and families deserved to benefit from public-health programs as much as the unemployed did.

Table 15 outlines potential costs and benefits from Medicaid reform. These changes had both political and economic components. By introducing co-payments or sliding-scale premiums, legislators sought to provide additional revenue for subsidized health insurance not only out of economic necessity but also because beneficiary contributions could increase political support for programs within legislative chambers and among citizens. Legislators in Colorado, Tennessee, and Florida suggested that Medicaid failed politically because beneficiaries remained disengaged from using health services prudently and the program had no mechanisms to hold either providers or beneficiaries accountable for inefficient service utilization.

Background

Medicaid presented the mirror image of the problems legislators associated with undependable revenues discussed in chapter 3. Exorbitant annual increases in Medicaid appropriations created repeated fiscal crises in which representatives cut nonhealth spending or raised taxes. Between 1987 and 1993, Medicaid spending rose from less than 10 percent of all state government spending to nearly 18 percent (Council of State Governments 1994). In Tennessee, Medicaid expenditures doubled from $820 million in 1987 to $1.6 billion in 1991, and these increases nearly bankrupted the state general fund (Tennessee 1994–95). Legislators in other states faced less severe crises, but cost increases nonetheless motivated efforts to change the Medicaid program.

Along with rising costs, Medicaid has suffered from other unintended, related problems. Foremost among these is that general-practice physicians have declined to accept Medicaid patients as reimbursement fees provided by the program have fallen below those paid by private, paying patients. Consequently, an increasing proportion of beneficiaries have sought health services in hospital emergency rooms, thereby requiring Medicaid to pay higher reimbursements to hospitals than would have been

TABLE 15.   Costs and Benefits of Medicaid Reform

Constituency	Benefits	Costs
Current medicaid beneficiaries	Doctor–patient relationship	Co-pays
	Preventive services	Sliding-scale premiums
Working uninsured	Insurance coverage Doctor–patient relationship	Co-pays Sliding-scale premiums
Insured citizens	Preventive services Reduced cost shifting from uncompensated and partially compensated care	Higher sin taxes
		Possible increase in cost shifting from utilization of health services by formerly uninsured
	Fewer reductions in and more dependable nonhealth government services	
	Lower taxes conditioned on Medicaid savings	

paid to physicians. Legislators recognized that because federal Medicaid guidelines prohibited co-payments from beneficiaries, families had no incentive to seek physician care prior to seeking emergency-room care. This dilemma further compounded Medicaid cost increases.

Representatives identified Medicaid as the federal-state programs in which they had lost the greatest policy latitude and in which federal mandates imposed the highest costs. Twenty-seven percent of the legislators interviewed cited Medicaid as the most costly intergovernmental program and as a program in which mandates drove costs.[3] A Colorado legislator summarized the overall effects of Medicaid mandates:

> *Representative:* Government mandating has really had an adverse effect on the Colorado state government—particularly . . . in health care. Really, Medicaid has been driving the state budget for the last seven or eight years. In 1986, we spent $364 million on Medicaid. Now that figure is $1.3 billion. Now, that's a lot of money that could be going to education. . . . The penny on the sales tax was for what? $300 million?
>
> *GB:* $364 million.
>
> *Representative:* Right, $364 million. Even after inflation, the increase in Medicaid is probably at most $600 million but not $900 million over eight years. So all that money could have gone to education, and we wouldn't have gone to the voters only to get turned down anyway on the sales tax.

From 1966 through 1985, relatively high medical inflation created three-quarters of Medicaid costs increases. By the mid-1980s, an increasing percentage of cost increases resulted from federal requirements that states enroll more beneficiaries based on particular categories of need (U.S. Advisory Commission 1992, 12). These enrollment increases became acute during the 1990 recession and began to place tremendous pressure on state budgets at a time when many states faced declining revenues. At the same time, the federal government did not identify Medicaid mandates as unfunded mandates in the same way as environmental regulations. Medicaid regulations were categorized as conditions for aid.

Legislators found skyrocketing expenditures forcing them to reshape health-care policies. These costs impinged on their ability to provide other goods and services, including education and training, anticrime measures, and tax reductions. Faced with the prospect of providing ever-more-expensive benefits to a group of people many voters viewed as undeserving, legislators moved to control the costs of the program lest all citizens find their benefit/tax ratios continually declining. Seventy percent of legislators discussed how accelerating Medicaid expenditure increases influenced their support for health-care reform. Half of the legislators identified specific non–health related spending cuts and tax increases that had been enacted because of Medicaid costs.

Thirty-three of seventy-six legislators who discussed health reforms indicated that they supported transforming health benefits because they did not believe that Medicaid delivered benefits to those who deserved them. Beyond the issue of cost savings was the issue of offering government goods and services that accord with legislators' principles about who should benefit from government spending.

Although concerns about rising Medicaid appropriations provided the primary motivation for reform efforts, two other factors encouraged representatives. First, problems in private insurance markets prodded Republicans to support changes in health-care and insurance packages. Legislatures in Colorado, Florida, Washington, Oregon, and New York have all addressed issues such as preexisting conditions, insurance portability, and insurance rating systems. Second, a lack of political support for Medicaid encouraged some Republicans and many Democrats to promote Medicaid changes to generate greater support for broad health-care reforms.

Legislators developed reform packages based on legislative political dynamics, governors' leadership, available financial resources, and extent of the Medicaid crisis in their states. Legislators referred frequently to equity issues and invoked the ability-to-pay and deserves-to-pay principles. A third variation of the equity principles was that certain citizens deserved to benefit from state public-health programs. Legislators suggested that children and the working poor deserved as much assistance in obtaining health insurance as did current Medicaid beneficiaries. Legislators addressed concerns about vertical transferability, dependability, and, to a lesser extent, obscurability.

Strategies for Health-Care Reform

State reforms shared a common denominator in their efforts to transform Medicaid from a particular-benefits program into a program more closely resembling a public good. Medicaid offered particular benefits by paying on a fee-for-service basis. Consequently, the distribution of benefits depended first on eligibility for Medicaid and then on an individual's utilization of health services. In contrast, most of the state reform plans abandoned individual services and moved to subsidies for insurance policies or membership in health maintenance organizations (HMOs), with the ultimate goal of insuring the entire state population. By 1993, sixteen states used managed-care programs for basic Medicaid services to the nonelderly (U.S. Advisory Commission 1993).

In the managed-care programs, insurance policies became the benefits for citizens. Individual policy premiums and coverage determined benefits and costs for enrollees. The extent of coverage and subsidy rates among Medicaid and uninsured populations determined the cost to the state and federal governments. These new programs more closely resembled a public good in that eligibility was no longer restricted by employment but was instead determined by income or ability to pay. Although no state offered universal coverage, the states' new roles as the insurers of last resort meant that citizens who lost private insurance could turn to the state program. Legislators sought to make health insurance a public good through which everyone would have an insurance policy for which they would pay according to a combination of their ability and their utilization of health services (i.e., a combination of the ability-to-pay and deserves-to-pay principles). In contrast to other public goods such as national defense, insurance coverage would be produced both publicly via state subsidies and privately via HMOs and private insurers. The transformed Medicaid program became analogous to public goods, such as education, that are produced via both private and public means but are nonetheless available to and consumed by all citizens.

A few basic ingredients were more or less present in state reform strategies. Legislators fostered bipartisan support for reform by offering Republicans and Democrats means to improve the well-being of disparate groups of citizens with a single reform package. Legislators recognized the incremental nature of policy change and pursued modest progress toward cost containment and increased coverage over and above their goals for either universal coverage (favored by Democrats) or a more privately based, free-enterprise health system (favored by Republicans). Incremental policy change also offered an avenue by which legislators could rebuild support for public-health programs, which had eroded. A third component emerged when state officials negotiated federal waivers in which they could generate efficiencies in Medicaid and retain any savings.

Other strategic considerations emerged. Politically, legislators considered the willingness of the governor to invest political capital in health-care reform, the prospects for federal health-care reform, and the necessity and probability of attracting bipartisan support. From a policy perspective, reform architects contemplated how far they could expand insurance coverage and the necessity of reform itself, a consideration driven by the extent of the state's Medicaid crisis.[4] With these concerns in mind, legislators in six states made serious efforts to alter their Medicaid programs and health-care systems.

The legislative proposals in Colorado, Florida, Tennessee, Oregon, Vermont, and Washington illustrate how health-care reform was an effort to transform a particular-benefits program into a public good and was shaped by federal policies and politics and how the tax alternatives available to legislators set parameters for their proposals.

Medicaid: Managed Reform

The efforts to transform Medicaid from a fee-for-service program to a subsidized managed-care program represent a shift from a particular-benefits program to a program more closely resembling a public good. With managed-care proposals, the benefits become either a state-subsidized insurance policy or membership in an HMO. Whereas beneficiaries' utilization of health services represented the value of benefits under Medicaid, the cost of an insurance policy or HMO membership represents the value of benefits with the managed-care programs.

The assertion that health-care reforms changed Medicaid from a particular-benefits program to one more closely resembling a public good deserves further explanation. Only in Washington and Oregon did legislators enact programs designed to provide universal coverage in a comprehensive legislative package. In the other states, a considerable portion of a state's uninsured population would remain uninsured. Nonetheless, every reform package moved away from Medicaid, which strictly limited health services to specific groups, such as the indigent elderly and single, unemployed parents and their children. In its place, subsidized managed care broadened the population served and moved toward a situation in which health insurance, not health services, would become a nonexclusionary public good.

Tennessee. The movement to managed care received considerable bipartisan support among legislators. Representatives offered bipartisan support for the movement because of its potential cost savings. Democrats stressed that the shift enabled them to offer health insurance to a greater number of individuals than Medicaid could. Republicans supported expanded coverage and the opportunity to decrease cost shifting by health-care providers.[5]

Among the case-study states, only Tennessee authorized wholesale reform in a single legislative session. The legislature effectively exempted itself from the reform process when it enacted the hospital tax in 1992 and required that the tax expire in 1994. At that time, the Medicaid replacement program was to be enacted or the state would revert to using sales tax revenues for Medicaid appropriations. Despite the lack of a formal legislative role, several legislators involved themselves in the development of Tenncare, the state's managed-care replacement for Medicaid. Although the governor could enact Tenncare without further legislation, he needed some level of legislative acceptance because legislators would appropriate funds for Tenncare and thus play a role in its administration and political viability.

Tennessee representatives commented that both the financial and political problems with Medicaid motivated them to demand its replacement. Legislators believed that increasing taxes to continually fuel Medicaid spending was not sustainable because the program had lost too much political support. In other words, Medicaid had lost both the political and policy accountability necessary for legislators to fund it. One Republican summarized the situation as follows:

> When we hit our crisis two years ago, I called the commissioner and asked him what we should do. He told me point blank, "This Medicaid is broken, and if I were you, I wouldn't dump any more money into it—not even what you have now, because you'll cut benefits every year. . . . So we had to do something to save money and to get the benefits out there more fairly.

The Tennessee legislature's response to the Medicaid funding crisis in 1992 illustrates federalism's creative politics. Initially Tennessee attempted to address its Medicaid funding crisis by taxing hospitals for Medicaid services and other indigent care. The legislature dedicated these revenues as the state source for Medicaid funding. This created a situation in which the state generated revenues from its own spending. The hospital tax enabled the state to attract federal matching grants for its Medicaid dollars by cycling the same state dollars through the program. For example, the federal government offers Tennessee approximately two dollars for every dollar it spends on Medicaid. If a service costs one hundred dollars and Tennessee taxes it at 50 percent, the price of the service rises to $150, of which Tennessee must pay $50 and the federal government $100. However, of the $150 spent, $100 went to cover the actual cost of the service, and $50 was remitted to the state government for the hospital tax. Table 16 depicts how Tennessee effectively recycled the same state dollars through its Medicaid program and essentially shifted the entire service cost of Medicaid to the federal government.

TABLE 16.   The Tennessee Indigent Services Tax

1	2	3	4
A: No Services Tax			
Patient • cost: 0 • benefit: $100	*Hospital* • cost: $100 • Revenue: $100 from Tennessee government	*Tennessee* • cost: $100 paid to hospital • Revenue: $67 from federal government; $33 from Tennessee taxpayers	*Federal government* • $67 to Tennessee *Tennessee taxpayers* • $33 to Medicaid
B: Indigent Services Tax			
Patient • cost: 0 • benefit: $100	*Hospital* • cost: $150 ($100 for service; $50 tax remitted to state government)	*Tennessee* • cost: $150 remitted to hospital • Revenue: $100 from federal government (67% of $150); $50 from hospital; nothing from taxpayers	*Federal government* • cost: $100 remitted to Tennessee (67% of $150) *Tennessee taxpayers* • cost: 0

This policy design enabled Tennessee to develop a system in which the federal government bore nearly 100 percent of Medicaid costs. When I asked why they abandoned this tax for the broader hospital tax, one legislator summarized his colleagues' responses:

> We moved from what we called Scam 1 to . . . Son of Scam, only because the feds came down on us for it. They didn't mind us doing it, but other states started to copy it. Hey, they were ready to go with it in Arkansas, so we had to have the broader hospital tax.

The legislature replaced the indigent-care tax with a broader 6.75 percent tax on all hospital services. Legislators supported the hospital tax because they perceived they could not raise the state's 8 percent sales tax or expand its base without dire political consequences. Five of the representatives interviewed related that many legislators would have preferred a broad-based tax instead of the hospital tax. Because the hospital tax fell on those who used health services, several representatives felt its incidence was inequitable. Nonetheless, the relatively high sales tax and constitutional prohibition against an income tax left the legislature with few options for broad-based taxes. Moreover, six legislators suggested that raising another tax would have only been the first in a never-ending series of tax increases if the state government did not address the underlying problem of increasing Medicaid costs. The obscurability and dependability of the hospital tax, coupled with its expiration, engendered sufficient support from both Republicans and Democrats.[6]

Although federal Medicaid mandates were conditions for aid rather than unfunded mandates, Tennessee's state government estimated the marginal cost to its treasury from changes in federal program requirements and funding. For its 1994 budget, Tennessee estimated that $206 million of $263 million in federally mandated expenditures occurred in Medicaid. However, $72 million of the $206 million were costs generated by decreases in the federal matching rate for Tennessee resulting from the state's economic growth.

Only in Tennessee did legislators never mention increasing tobacco and alcohol taxes. Not a single legislator indicated support for changing tobacco or liquor taxes, which may not be surprising given that Tennesseeans produce both products. Legislators either supported the hospital tax or stated that it was the least objectionable funding mechanism available in 1992 immediately following the voters' rejection of Governor

Ned McWherter's income tax proposal. Representatives rejected other tax increases because of low-tax philosophies or because such increases would have been the first in a series necessary to continue funding Medicaid in the absence of reform.

Despite the hospital tax's shortcomings, legislators saw advantages to it. The tax indirectly addressed cost shifting in health-care services. Federally determined reimbursement rates often fall below the actual cost of a service. As a result, service providers shifted the Medicaid costs onto private, paying patients. Thus, if Medicaid pays $50 for a service that costs $100, the hospital will charge a privately insured patient $150 for the same service. The hospital tax offered a limited response to cost shifting. By generating Medicaid dollars by taxing health services, legislators created a system in which greater cost shifting generated greater state Medicaid revenues, which were then matched two to one by the federal government. Greater Medicaid funding implied that the state could offer greater reimbursements for health services, thus decreasing the amount of uncompensated care.

Tennessee legislators enjoyed considerable success in setting the stage on which their state's Medicaid program was transformed into from a particular-benefits program to one more closely resembling a public good. After the program's enactment in March 1994, one-quarter of the state's uninsured and all of its Medicaid beneficiaries enrolled in Tenncare (Tennessee 1994–95).

In Tennessee, the legislature's actions in 1992 effectively exempted it from a formal role in reforming Medicaid. Several legislators commented that they took this step to ensure that the reform process did not unravel as lobbyists and legislators manipulated various components of reform packages. The Tennesseeans felt that the critical nature of their Medicaid crisis necessitated the relatively quick enactment of wholesale reform. The strategy succeeded to the extent that Tennessee abandoned Medicaid for Tenncare. The Tennessee strategy proved prudent, in contrast to events in Florida, where a last-minute Republican-led filibuster in the state senate derailed health-care reform.

Florida. The Florida House of Representatives passed the Florida Health Reform Act of 1994 by an overwhelming vote of 117 to 3. Two months later, Senate Democrats were unable to block a Republican-led filibuster, and the act failed to become law. The strategies behind the bipartisan support in the House were similar to those in other states. Rep-

resentatives built on the Basic Health Act of 1993, and Democratic committee chairpersons coupled insurance reform with a managed-care Medicaid alternative and offered cost savings. Additionally, the Committee on
Health specifically addressed Republican concerns about physician choice
by including an "any willing provider" clause that stipulated that managed-care enrollees could go to the physician of their choice but would
bear any costs above a state-determined reimbursement level. As one
influential Democrat with health-care expertise outlined,

> We've had to go back and forth, but basically we couldn't impose a
> tax to do it. We went to the hospitals, and they said they couldn't be
> pushed any further. But we knew that if you can get the working poor
> to contribute to something plus some share of a state subsidy, which
> we could afford by getting Medicaid recipients out of the [emergency
> rooms] and to the [general practitioners], then the state would be able
> to draw down the federal dollars to get the program going from the
> former Medicaid match.
>
> The next thing we offered them was Medicaid savings, and then we
> had the support for the plan, which passed through the House 117 to
> 3. Now I'm a little worried because Bob Dole is starting to send sig-
> nals to scuttle this in the [state] Senate.

Lobbyists and staffers confirmed that Senator Dole was involved in
the Florida legislation and speculated that he did not want states passing
efforts similar to President Clinton's national proposal. Activists from
both parties stated flatly that the Health Care Reform Act would have
given Governor Lawton Chiles a large boost in his tight reelection race.

As with the national debate on health reform, critics charged that
state efforts could lead to a decrease in choices among health services for
people enrolling in state-subsidized health-care plans. Republicans and
Democrats countered this charge with several arguments. Because the
state was paying most of the bill for those who relied on the state for insurance subsidies, it could justify limiting their choice of physicians. Most legislators intended for state-subsidized managed care programs to designate
"gatekeeper" general practitioners whom beneficiaries would visit prior to
receiving further services. Democrats responded that those on Medicaid
and those without health insurance relied too heavily on emergency-room
visits. Moving such persons from emergency rooms to physicians' offices

implied no decrease in choice. Third, supporters argued that the national politicians opposing reform because of decreasing choices were wrong.

A Florida Democrat noted that both Democratic and Republican opponents of the Florida Health Plan raised the issue of physician choice. In contrast to other states, where legislators attempted to counter the validity of the choice argument, Democrats on the health committee in the Florida House worked to accommodate the opposition's views.

> We have a certain section [of the legislature], mainly the Republicans, who would oppose everything and anything we would put on the table, so we said, "Why are you against this?" and they said, "It destroys choice." So we began from there and offered the "any willing provider" clause as a compromise on choice that enrollees could go to a [preferred-provider-organization] system if they pay for it, which puts them in a more traditional full-indemnity plan.

In Florida, a House Republican with a professional background in health care enlisted the support of the governor and his colleagues for a twenty-five-cents-per-pack cigarette tax to finance expanded coverage and offer new community health programs focusing on prevention. The tax climates in most states left legislators with few, if any, options for financing reform other than sin taxes. One Florida legislator offered his own assessment while enjoying a series of cigarettes:

> As much as we'd like to move on health reform, we really have no options to get the money for it. We can't raise taxes, and we only have the sales tax. The one exception is that we might get a cigarette tax. Hell, I just might be smoking the state to health right now. I've never thought of this habit as a public service before.

In most states, health-care reform proceeded incrementally. The Florida Health Security Act of 1994 followed on the heels of the Basic Health Act in 1993, although the former failed to become law. In Oregon, the legislature enacted the comprehensive Oregon Health Plan in 1989 but allowed itself opportunities to modify the plan over time by phasing in different elements. This incremental approach also afforded the state critical time to negotiate various waivers from federal laws. This federal role eventually placed a constraint on further implementation of the plan in 1995.

Oregon.   Oregon's recent experience with health reform indicates the limits the federal government can place on reform. Having gained several waivers to change its Medicaid program during the late 1980s and early 1990s, the Oregon legislature found it could not enact one of the final components of its reform package in 1995 because of the U.S. Congress's unwillingness to grant a waiver from the Employment and Retirement Income Security Act (ERISA). The legislature requested the waiver to enact a mandate that all employers offer a minimum insurance-benefits package to their employees. Although many Republicans opposed the mandates, several supported them. One senior Republican stated his reasons for supporting the measure, which had drawn widespread criticism in the national health-care debate the previous year:

> I'm troubled by the fact that in Oregon there are employers who don't want to pay for health insurance. It should be a part of doing business. I'm a small businessman, and it's unfair that I bear that cost in my pricing but my competitor won't, because then I pay again when my competitor's employees go and get uncompensated care. I think in Oregon we can move to universal coverage. I think we should.

With the support of several Republicans and most Democrats, Oregon legislators felt there was some likelihood of enacting an employer mandate. However, the issue became moot when Senator Robert Packwood passed the word that Congress was unlikely to grant the waiver. Republicans and Democrats recognized the irony that the Republican Congress that emphasized allowing states greater latitude for policy innovations would not grant a waiver for Oregon to reform its health-care system. One Republican suggested that his counterparts in Congress had no interest in granting a waiver from a federal mandate that would allow a state to enact a "Clinton-style" mandate that might work in the particular context of Oregon's health system.

Several Oregon representatives mentioned a dilemma that their incremental approach created in conjunction with the prospect of not receiving a congressional waiver from ERISA. By creating a state program to provide low-cost insurance to individuals but not placing an onus on employers to either provide such insurance or contribute to the state fund for it, legislators worried that they would make Oregon a health-care magnet: firms would locate in Oregon offering low- to medium-wage jobs without health-insurance benefits and then direct their employees to seek assistance obtaining health insurance from the state. The system would consequently be strained by the increasing demands on it.

The Oregon experience with health care was one in which a bipartisan group of lawmakers in both legislative chambers built support for health-care reform by promoting incremental changes each biennium and by detailing both savings from the changes and safeguards that would allow the state to contain costs if they began to skyrocket, as they had with Medicaid. Several legislators commented on the credibility Governor John Kitzhaber had developed on the issue by working with Republican legislators on the Oregon Health Plan as early as 1987.

Vermont. In some instances, the content of policy alternatives and their merits mattered less than the political appeals of promoting or opposing changes in Medicaid. A senior Republican Vermont legislator who favored shifting Medicaid to a managed-care program told me how his colleagues complained that the bipartisan reform compromise he promoted had too many benefits for their tastes:

> I kept telling them [that] to get the waiver, we can only trim so much from what we're now offering, and they'd keep saying the benefits in managed care were too generous. And I'd say, "But we have fewer benefits in that than we do in the current fee-for-service Medicaid, you dummies!"

Vermont legislators failed to enact a sweeping health-care reform package in 1993. Many attributed much of the failure to the legislature's inability to agree on a funding mechanism for the package (Pear 1994b). In 1995 the House passed a bill to provide subsidies for managed-care memberships to between 20 and 25 percent of the state's sixty thousand uninsured individuals. Republicans and Democrats supported a modest increase in tobacco taxes as the principal funding mechanism with the realization that the Republican-controlled Senate would accept only this tax change and that they could scale it back so that insurance might be offered to between five thousand and eight thousand people.

Washington. In Washington, legislators passed comprehensive health-care reform in 1993 that built on the state's Basic Health Act of 1987. In

1993 the legislature mandated that all employers offer health insurance to their employees by July 1995 and subsidized costs for small-business employers with tobacco, alcohol, and gasoline taxes.

Most Democrats and several Republicans supported these sin-tax increases. Later in 1993, however, Initiative 601 called for their repeal, thereby leaving health financing in peril. In response, several moderate Republicans developed and spearheaded the drive for Initiative 602, which limited the future growth of government but left the 1993 tax increases intact.

Sponsors of Initiative 602 suggested that they did not want to derail health reforms.[7] Given the initial popularity of Initiative 601 and the general "less government, lower taxes" mood pervading the state, the architects of Initiative 602 recognized the political necessity of offering an alternative initiative if the state was to have any resources with which to move forward with health-care reform. Thus, Initiative 602 preserved current revenues but limited future growth. In the absence of Initiative 602, legislators feared that Initiative 601 would pass and they would lose the health-reform funding.

Supporters of Initiatives 601 and 602 agreed that the strategy for Initiative 602 worked. Initiative 601 failed, and Initiative 602 passed narrowly. One of the architects of Initiative 601 noted that his plan had enjoyed broad support until Initiative 602 was introduced. Shortly before the election, the revelation that tobacco companies heavily financed advertising in support of Initiative 601 further eroded its support. Legislators agreed that this decline at least implicitly promoted Initiative 602.

Colorado.   As in Washington, the citizen referendum process played a role in legislators' support for health-care reform in Colorado. The state began planning for health-care reform under the rubric of Amendment 1, which limited state and local spending and subjected tax changes to a statewide vote. This provision dampened legislators' enthusiasm for any reform plan that could not be enacted on a pay-as-you-go basis within the existing tax structure. Republican and Democratic legislators complained that even if they could guarantee savings with a managed-care alternative to Medicaid, they could not support any proposal that included new taxes or fees that would be subject to a statewide vote. As one Democrat noted, "We don't want to start anything new because no matter how good it may be or [even if] we can cut other taxes a year from now, if we try to do anything involving money Doug Bruce [the leader of the antitax movement] sues you."[8]

Some Republicans initially opposed Governor Roy Roemer's managed-care plan on the grounds that it limited physician choice. But this argument lost steam in Colorado when leading Republicans argued that the cost savings from Colorado Care could offset any loss of physician choice among Medicaid beneficiaries and that physician choice was either nonexistent or not a priority for Medicaid beneficiaries. One Colorado Republican stated that he felt nationally prominent Republicans were performing a disservice to Republican state legislators who needed to find Medicaid savings to balance their budgets. He explained:

> On the issue of choice—that's really a Trojan horse to talk about preserving the status quo. Besides what you may hear from the national parties, managed care does not mean you won't have any choice in health care. You can choose your managed-care network, and these may be employer based in many cases. Now the only choices you have are who your employer enrolls with or what plans they sponsor, and people are getting pulled away from their physicians by their employers. I see managed care as a means of unraveling some of that dilemma.

The overriding reason Coloradans gave for moving away from Colorado Care was that in early 1994 the Medicaid funding crisis abated for the first time in eight years. By February 1994, the Republican chairperson of the House Appropriations Committee had announced that Medicaid expenditures would fall $200 million below projections because of lower-than-expected medical inflation and an overall improvement in the state's labor market. This windfall decreased the necessity of shepherding a contentious program through a legislature controlled by a slim Republican majority and presenting it to a Democratic governor. With a divided legislature and a contentious issue, representatives from both parties indicated that they preferred to wait until after the 1994 elections to grapple with health care.

Discussion

The debate over health care has developed many elements at both the national and subnational levels. Three of these elements are of particular interest with respect to benefit/tax ratios and the role of representatives in changing the economic and physical well-being of their constituents. First, legislators seek to maximize their constituents' benefit/tax ratios and will not tolerate a program that consistently decreases those ratios. Lawmakers will offer policy changes when a government program clearly lowers the benefit/tax ratios of a majority of citizens, as was the case with Medicaid, where large, persistent cost increases necessitated cuts in other programs or tax increases. Just as legislators pursue revenue dependability, they also seek spending regularity.

Second, tax options matter. Legislators change policies when they perceive constituents are not well served by them. If constituents will not tolerate further tax increases for programs or perceive that they unfairly benefit certain groups of citizens, legislators will act to remedy the situation. In such cases, legislators act not just as revenue maximizers but as agents for citizens' utility maximization. In the case of health care, most legislators felt that they could not justify changing broad-based taxes to pay for Medicaid reforms and thus supported increasing alcohol and tobacco taxes as the only viable alternative.

Although state representatives favored expanding health coverage and saving money, their willingness to tap new revenue sources to provide subsidies restricted the scope of their reforms. No legislator indicated a willingness to raise either income or sales taxes to finance health-care reform, although several Vermont legislators hoped that the state might do so after a managed-care program restored public confidence in public-health programs. With pressure to cut taxes, resolve local property tax issues, and fulfill various mandates, legislators found that they had little latitude to finance Medicaid reform. Consequently, legislators in nearly every state turned to sin taxes as the only viable route. Among the legislators who commented specifically on sin taxes, thirty-four indicated support, while six Republicans opposed any tax increases as part of their limited-government philosophies.

A third element in the debate over health care that is germane to benefit/tax ratios and representatives' roles in changing them regards federal politics. From a policy perspective, the waivers granted or denied by Congress, the Health Care Financing Administration, and the Clinton and Bush administrations created the parameters for state health reform. From a political perspective, the relationships among officeholders at the state and federal levels influenced both the direction for health reforms and the enthusiasm with which various groups either promoted or opposed reform. In this federal context, representatives attempted to build support for transforming Medicaid and sought adequate revenues to finance their reform proposals.

Federal laws and politicians played important roles in state health-care reform. Federal regulations administered primarily by the Health Care Financing Administration guided both the timing and the parameters of state-proposed Medicaid changes. The ability of state legislators and administrators to convince federal officials to grant Medicaid waivers determined the structure of state reform. Politically, legislators' and governors' relationship with members of Congress and President Clinton played a role in encouraging reform in Tennessee and to a lesser extent in Washington.

Finally, the nature of the program—whether it is a particular-benefits program or a public-good—matters not only in economics but also in politics. The particular benefits provided by Medicaid and to whom they were provided contributed to its lack of political accountability. Legislators hope that the public-good (i.e., less exclusionary) nature of state-subsidized managed-care policies will expand the scope of coverage and address the deserves-to-pay principle sufficiently to engender support for new public-health-assistance programs.

Chapter 8

Conclusion

Federalism creates new politics. In addition to structural and institutional relationships, models of intergovernmental relations and subnational politics should consider the political spillover through which politics shifts from one level of government to another. Investigations and models of subnational politics should consider the provision of public goods in federal systems and how the unique nature of public goods affects subnational policy. It is important to investigate how perceptions, principles, and goals of actors in subnational governments shape state politics and form public policy in an intergovernmental context. The case studies provide direct observation of these components of state politics and, consequently, improve the understanding of state politics. There is now a better understanding of the changes in state politics caused by the unique role of governments in providing public goods and the structural and less formal relationships among governments.

This chapter ties together the case studies and collective decisions from the eleven states concerning taxes, economic development, education, and Medicaid. Following a few general conclusions, there are two sections. First, I provide an analysis of the relationships among policies and comparisons of the four policy areas. This analysis contrasts how legislators perceive different policies. Moreover, it indicates linkages among policies that are not typically captured in analyses of state politics focusing on a single policy. The case-study approach enables comprehension of how state politicians link not only taxes and services generally but also economic development, health care, and education to one another.

Following the policy comparisons, I compare states and discern how differences among them produced different policy decisions. I then close with insights about the case-study method. As with the comparative policy analysis, the state case studies offer an opportunity to understand how

combinations of variables (e.g., party and state constitutional limits) interact to produce politics and policies. In this sense, the case studies open the
black box of empirical models of politics and enable understanding of how
legislatures arrive at collective decisions rather than only what components contributed to those decisions.

Differences across policies are produced by variances in the perceptions about whether the policy produces a public good, a mixed good, or
particular benefits; in the extent and nature of the financial crisis created
by an existing policy; and in the intergovernmental arrangements and
avenues available to address a specific policy problem. Differences across
states are produced by differences in responses to national politics, in partisan politics and ideology, in policy history, and in the legislatures' powers and abilities to respond to specific policy problems.

Policy Connections and Conclusions

Several conclusions can be drawn from the case studies examining taxes,
economic development, education, and health care. Although no formal
supply-side mechanism exists to determine the supply and pricing of public goods, state legislators adapt to their institutional environments and
rely on a fairly stable set of principles when enacting tax policy. In conjunction with these principles, individual perceptions about what is a public good, state constitutions requiring the provision of certain goods, and
legislators' willingness to engage the avenues of federalism all influence
what services governments provide and how they provide them.

Among all the policies, taxes were omnipresent. In and of itself, this is
unsurprising. Less obviously, taxes constrained and created opportunities
for policy alternatives for economic development, education, and health
care. Tennessee, Washington, and New York identified broad tax reforms
as the best, albeit implicit, economic-development policies they could
engage, yet the political risks and fiscal costs of doing so made such policy
changes nearly impossible to pursue.

State representatives entered the nebulous range in which both taxes
and benefits move unidirectionally, but when they did so they safeguarded
their moves by promoting programs for which they perceived support or
by obfuscating the taxes they imposed. In Michigan, legislators recognized
that after Governor John Engler's two failed attempts at property tax
reform, they could safely promote a tax trade in which citizens could voice
their support for either an income or a sales tax rather than blame the leg-

islature for the choice. In Tennessee, representatives recognized the lack of support for Medicaid, enacted the hospital tax to provide temporary funding, and technically exempted themselves from the Medicaid reform process so that voters could not blame them should Tenncare fail. In Florida, Vermont, and Washington, legislators connected health-reform proposals to taxes on alcohol and tobacco products rather than risk voter antipathy for financing a discredited program, Medicaid, or its replacement with general tax revenues beyond those already dedicated to it.

The constraints created by tax politics were most evident in state health-care-reform efforts. In every state considering health care reform—Tennessee, Florida, Colorado, Vermont, Oregon, and Washington—representatives declined to consider broad-based tax changes as a means of expanding subsidized health-insurance coverage to the working poor. The interactions among 1990s tax politics and the lack of policy accountability for Medicaid restricted opportunities for reform, and legislators employed the deserves-to-pay principle in efforts to generate marginal revenues for modest expansions of subsidized insurance programs for the working poor.

In the U.S. federal system, tax politics dominated state politics because of vertical tax base competition as much as horizontal rate competition among states. Legislators reported consistently that resentment toward the federal income tax fueled their constituents' antitax sentiments. The lawmakers responded by promoting relatively obscure and incremental state sales taxes. Mississippi and Michigan representatives exemplified this response, and similar concerns about income tax reductions surfaced in New Jersey, Oregon, Massachusetts, New York, and Vermont. Even in Vermont, where legislators voted for a sales tax decrease instead of an income tax cut, many legislators indicated a preference for the income tax decrease. Other Vermont legislators preferred the sales tax reduction but suggested that they would raise sales taxes before income taxes in the event a tax increase became necessary. Ultimately, Vermont representatives perceived that they could retain a higher sales tax to fund education and property tax reform, but they could not do so to finance an expanded Medicaid/insurance subsidy program.

In ten of the states, legislators unequivocally saw economic development and education as directly linked, but they differed in how. In the eleventh state, Mississippi, most legislators identified education as a component in economic development, but a minority of representatives also cited the brain-drain problem. In Washington, Oregon, Tennessee, New Jersey, and Michigan, representatives suggested that the most potent link between education and economic development was in community colleges offering specific vocational skills. These community colleges become a community resource available to retrain workers as labor markets change. Massachusetts General Court and New York assembly members took a more elitist view of education, suggesting that the research universities in their states were the new "anchor employers" for attracting high-skilled, high-wage workers.

The connection between economic development and health care was implicit and counterproductive. In all eleven states, representatives argued that escalating Medicaid costs implicitly kept tax rates high and forced the legislatures to shift dollars from public-goods development programs such as education and infrastructure to pay for Medicaid cost increases. In some states—Colorado, for example—Medicaid spending had grown nearly fourfold from the mid-1980s through the mid-1990s.

National tax politics did not preclude legislatures from enacting large tax increases to assume greater financial responsibility for local public education but did shape the taxes legislators invoked to pay for education. No state enacted an income tax increase to finance additional education spending, and Michigan used its assumption of local property taxes to cut income taxes modestly. Only Oregon's legislature voted twice to withhold income tax rebates to comply with court orders to equalize education funding. Michigan and Mississippi voted 2 percent and 1 percent sales tax increases, respectively, to finance education. The Vermont legislature delayed a sales tax decrease to provide school property tax relief. In contrast, Colorado voted against a sales tax increase dedicated to increasing primary and secondary education.

The sharpest contrast among the policies took place between health care and education—the two policies that best represent particular benefits and public goods. In six states, legislatures found the resources necessary to equalize funding across local school districts for education. In three states—New Jersey, Massachusetts, and Oregon—the legislature acted with the knowledge that failing to do so would result in court interventions. But in three other states—Michigan, Mississippi, and Vermont—the state houses responded to political demands for reform, and no legislator perceived dire political costs from raising state taxes to ameliorate a local problem.

Education politics in Massachusetts, Vermont, New Jersey, Oregon, Mississippi, and Tennessee indicated subnational politicians' willingness to engage in redistributive policy-making. The redistributive policies ameliorated discrepancies in local resources and were not direct income transfers. Because of the different parameters of education financing, state representatives might not be expected to worry about their states becoming education magnets in the same way they could become welfare magnets (Peterson and Rom 1990), yet there is still a willingness to ensure that poor areas receive adequate resources, even when the motivations for such actions come from courts or state constitutions. This suggests that subnational politics are less limited than other scholars have suggested (Peterson 1981; Dye 1990). Scholars have perhaps concluded prematurely that subnational politicians hesitate to engage in redistributive policy-making because they have focused primarily on redistribution among individuals and families, whereas state politicians focus on redistributive policies among local communities.

State representatives were substantially more guarded about expanding a redistributive particular-benefits program such as Medicaid. Nonetheless, the inequities in Medicaid coverage among unemployed and working poor families and household heads encouraged many representatives from Tennessee, Colorado, Oregon, Vermont, and Washington to promote limited reforms designed to incrementally expand insurance coverage. Concerns about equity within the state overrode concerns about the external effects of changing a redistributive program, and concerns about redistribution did not prevent legislators from enacting Medicaid reforms. Indeed, both Republican and Democratic representatives offered reform packages or voted in favor of some expansion of Medicaid or managed-care subsidies for the working poor. The problem was not an aversion to government redistribution. Rather, the problem was budget constraints and an unwillingness on the part of legislators to shift resources more than they already had or to increase taxes to generate marginal resources to support Medicaid expansion . Most legislators indicated that Medicaid or any replacement program would need to restore the policy accountability of public-health programs before considerable resources could be devoted to them.

With Medicaid, legislatures failed to enact reforms more frequently than with education. Florida found its health-care-reform package the victim of a filibuster, and Colorado declined to pursue health-care reform as the national debate degenerated and as its Medicaid crisis receded. In Oregon, where bipartisan support for expanding the state's health plan existed, the lack of a federal waiver constrained further efforts (somewhat the converse of the courts forcing states to change their education financing). In Vermont and Washington, legislatures scaled back reform efforts because of funding constraints and a paucity of tax options, hoping that restoring policy accountability to Medicaid might enable them to expand the program incrementally in the future. Only in Tennessee, where the legislature exempted itself from the reform process and where the sunset provision on the hospital-services tax necessitated reform, did a major overhaul of a state's Medicaid program transpire.

In contrast to education, there was less consensus about the nonexclusionary nature of health care, the appropriate private-public mix, and how to effectively respond to the Medicaid cost crisis. In Colorado, Vermont, and Florida, national health-care politics intruded on the state so that state reform efforts were withdrawn, scaled back, or failed. In Oregon, Washington, and Tennessee, national politics influenced state reform efforts less, but tax constraints nonetheless constrained reform efforts even when there was a bipartisan consensus on addressing the coverage discrepancies created by the current Medicaid system.

The comparisons among policies provide a different perspective from that of many studies of state politics, which compare states across time. One of the primary advantages of this approach is that in addition to better understanding both state politics and policies per se, there is also an understanding of the linkages among the policies within and across states. For example, it is easier to understand how Washington's and Tennessee's tax politics shape their approaches to economic-development policy and how New Jersey's dominant tax politics constrains its policy options for education financing. It is also possible to see how Mississippi's income tax system provides a tool for its economic-development efforts and how Tennessee has responded by instituting a rebate program in its relatively nominal business-franchise tax.

Differences across States

Before moving to conclusions based on the specific differences across states, it is important to note that the case studies about collective decision making enable an understanding of more than what components comprise state policies and the policy processes. The cases provide a better understanding of how proposals wend their way through legislative processes. Whereas other state policy analyses often offer some idea about the relative importance of independent influences, such as partisanship and ideology (Erikson, Wright, and McIver 1993), the cases provide illustrations of how these variables interacted in political arenas to produce both politics and policy outcomes. In many instances, these outcomes reflected legislative decisions not to act or to retain current policies. Direct observation of state politics allows analysis of such nondecisions and slicing into state politics in a way that is not possible when relying on variance in empirical data to provide the explanation.

A second important point about the case studies vis-à-vis empirical studies of state politics is that the cases rely less on retrospective data about state policy outputs and reveal more information about the actual policy process. Whereas studies of state-specific policies such as welfare (Plotnick and Winters 1985) and taxes (Garand 1988) analyze data after the legislatures have decided on policy alternatives, the state case studies enable better observation of why some alternatives survive while others whither.

Representatives had substantially different perceptions about public goods and about which level of government should provide them. Generally, legislators viewed public education as nonexclusionary, although opinions varied about whether state or local government should have responsibility for funding education. In Massachusetts, Michigan, Mississippi, and Vermont, legislators voted for the states to assume more responsibility for education as a means of addressing local resource disparities and placating voter dismay over property taxes. In these cases, legislative actions indicate two things. First, the means of taxation affects the political viability of financing public goods, with sales taxes currently being viewed as the least offensive and politically risky. The second indication involves legislators' perceptions about their roles as the middle layer of government in a federal system.

State representatives perceive that citizens view their tax burdens and their benefits as a collective bundle of goods and services. Consequently, state representatives worry about unpopular federal policies (e.g., income tax) and may seek to intervene to ameliorate unpopular or failing local policies. Doing so implies that state legislators will actively change citizens' benefit/tax ratios even when they are uncertain of the consequences of such policy changes for all their constituents.

In addition to legislators' governing principles and individual positions, four factors substantially influenced the states' collective decisions and policy changes or lack thereof. Policy histories, opportunities for citizen participation, court interventions and federal mandates, and party politics contributed to the variations in both whether states changed their tax, development, education, and health policies and the content of those policy changes.

The influence of policy histories was most evident in tax-policy changes. Enacting new taxes is more difficult than changing existing ones, and the tax-policy changes observed bear this out. In Tennessee and Washington, voters have repeatedly rejected income tax enactments, and by 1995, most legislators in those states perceived that expending further political capital on the issue was not worthwhile. Florida representatives reported that the botched 1986 services tax and their own repeated failures to rationalize and reform the sales tax left them far from the threshold where they might even propose an income tax. These lawmakers fully expected that voters would reject such a proposal. The only new tax enacted in a no-income-tax state was Tennessee's health-services tax, which was obscured, was borne by third-party payers, and expired after two years.

In contrast, changing existing taxes was much more frequent, and legislatures raised some taxes and reduced others, sometimes simultaneously. The Vermont legislature delayed a sales tax decrease, and the Oregon legislature twice voted to retain income tax rebates. The Mississippi legislature raised the state sales tax while enacting income tax reductions. In Michigan, the legislature provided voters with a choice of tax increases. Perhaps less surprisingly, assembly members in New Jersey and New York agreed to tax reductions—sizable in New Jersey and modest in New York.

Policy history and the interplay among policies became relevant in determining the various economic-development policies. Mississippi's income tax made its employer interest subsidy/individual income tax credit possible. Tennessee had no such provision and thus moved more toward a public-goods strategy for economic development. In education, Michigan representatives argued that their relatively low sales tax rate made raising it and decreasing income taxes politically and fiscally possible. In New Jersey, assembly members suggested that cutting the sales tax rate in 1992 may have given them the slack necessary to raise it later in the event they were forced to reform the state's property tax system.

Tax politics in Michigan and New Jersey indicated that the states' tax options influenced the options for property tax reforms. In Michigan, Republicans and Democrats banded together to convince the Republican governor of the need to offer an alternative to local property taxes and to emphasize the sales tax because it was low relative to other states and could be promoted using the concept of horizontal transferability. In New

Jersey, partisans from both sides contended that the disastrous Florio tax increase in 1990 meant that the state would not soon undertake large-scale property tax reform and that any tax rate increases would be targeted to the sales tax.

Citizen participation changed both policy contents and the political dynamics for representatives and their legislatures. In Michigan, the opportunity to present citizens with a choice between an income tax or sales tax increase and an assured property tax decrease presented legislators with a win-win situation. Michigan representatives, and perhaps the governor, learned from two previous ballot initiatives that voters would reject property tax reform measures that jeopardized school funding. This demonstrates not only that citizen participation can change politics between citizens and elites but also that repeated interactions may influence policy alternatives.

Oregon and Colorado voters rejected sales tax changes proposed in referenda. In Oregon, this rejection left representatives grappling with how to progress toward equal funding for education, a subject that dominated the 1995 session. In Colorado, the voters' rejection of a one cent increase in the sales tax had less dramatic fiscal effects and deprived the legislature of marginal revenues it would have appropriated for public education.

Courts and decisions by the federal government also create federal politics. Spurred by federal mandates for greater coverage, Tennessee completely redesigned its Medicaid program, the enactment of which, in turn, depended on the granting of federal waivers. Medicaid politics loomed large in Florida, Oregon, Washington, Colorado, and Vermont. Although not all states faced financial crisis, changing federal coverage regulations, increasing costs, and the states' abilities to negotiate waivers from Medicaid regulations shaped their pursuit of Medicaid reform.

Court intervention played a larger role in state and local politics. Direct intervention led to Governor James Florio's 1990 tax increase, which then created the antitax politics that permeated the state during the mid-1990s. Court decisions and oversight influenced legislative decisions for states to assume greater financial responsibility for education funding in Oregon, Washington, New Jersey, and Massachusetts. Representatives in Michigan and Vermont reported that if their legislatures had not acted, they likely would have had to respond to court mandates to change education funding.

State party politics played a variety of roles in collective policy decisions. Subtly, party politics often shaped the content of legislative alternatives. In Vermont, moderate Republicans and Democrats worked to develop bipartisan proposals for property tax reform that would pass the Democrat-controlled House and the Republican-controlled Senate. In Michigan, the bipartisan working group for tax reform convinced Governor John Engler to support a ballot initiative with a replacement tax for local property taxes. In Florida and Colorado, the need for bipartisan support for health-care legislation led a Republican committee chairperson in Colorado and a Democratic committee chairperson in Florida to link expansions of Medicaid to health-insurance reform.

Perhaps because party politics shaped policy options, divided government or unified party government did not especially affect whether a policy decision would be made, although it did affect the scope of policy change. New Jersey, with Republican supermajorities in both houses of its legislature and a Republican governor, voted for a 25 percent income tax cut. Tennessee's unified Democratic government voted to exempt itself from health-care reform and charged Governor Ned McWherter with creating a new Medicaid program that the legislature could not modify or reject. And Washington's unified Democratic government enacted health reform to insure the 7 percent of Washingtonians who lacked health coverage. Although Florida had a unified government, its legislature failed to enact health-care reform when Senate Republicans employed their minority filibuster power.

In contrast, New York's divided government voted for modest tax relief in 1994, and Vermont's divided government agreed to incremental reforms for both education finance and Medicaid. In Colorado, the Republican House declined to further consider health-care reform when a midyear budget report indicated that Medicaid expenditures would be $200 million below predictions and thus the state would run a surplus. Democratic and Republican legislators both suggested that the retreat would avoid a year-long negotiation with Democratic Governor Roy Roemer. Michigan's divided government enacted sweeping tax reform but did so in a way that placed responsibility on the voters.

Methods

These case studies demonstrate that many subtleties of subnational politics can best be understood via observation and case study. Unlike aggregate state spending and revenue data, case studies enable the examination of alternatives not chosen as well as of the consequences of chosen alternatives. The politics that lead legislators away from their most preferred policy position to moderated positions can be understood. At the level of collective decision making, the case studies enable an understanding of both policy changes and failed attempts at changing policy.

Although the case studies do not provide the precision of some models, using the metrics of benefit/tax ratios and changes in them permits analysis of subnational elected officials' policy calculations in the context of their political calculations. In some cases, such as tax increases and service reductions or tax decreases and service increases, the incentives and constraints on representatives are clear. But when services and taxes change unidirectionally, state representatives often face a nebulous task in deciding how to change policies to maximize constituent support for both the service and their own political fortunes.

The case studies from eleven states afford observation not just of annual policy changes but also of policy proposals that officeholders considered and ultimately either rejected or failed to enact. Without the benefit of direct observation, it would not be possible to see legislators' policy connections between government functions, such as education, and broader, general revenue taxes, such as sales taxes. Observers might also fail to understand which policies legislators believe they can promote in tandem with revenue increases. It would not be possible to see the initial motives behind Tennessee's indigent-health-services tax and the reasoning for connecting the more general hospital-services tax to Medicaid spending while the McWherter administration developed Tenncare. Scholars might also fail to see that the immediacy of the Medicaid problem in Tennessee encouraged many legislators to support the unusual move of exempting the legislature from a direct role in Tenncare's development.

A second example of how the interviews and case studies allow additional understanding of state politics comes from New York. From the standpoint of small-business profitability, many legislators could make compelling arguments for a reduction in the state's commercial utility taxes, yet the governor and Republican state senate leadership opted for a reduction in corporate-profits taxes, which would largely assist already profitable businesses. As such, the legislature and governor agreed to a tax cut in which many perceived that symbolism outweighed substantive policy considerations promoting alternative tax reductions.

To the extent that politics is the art of the possible, the case studies enable the observation of numerous possibilities that are not evident in final policies and are invisible in aggregate data on state spending and revenues. It would not be possible to see Vermont legislators negotiating when House Democrats bucked a national trend for a state income tax cut and instead enacted a sales tax cut, only to agree with the governor and Senate Republicans to delay the sales tax reduction to fully fund property tax relief programs. In Michigan, Democrats and Republicans confirmed that only through a series of meetings with the governor and his staff were they able to convince John Engler to campaign for a tax-neutral trade from property taxes to a sales tax. And in New York, aggregate data on taxes and even a legislative history would not have revealed some assembly members' preferences for reductions in the utility tax to promote economic development instead of the corporate-profits tax changes negotiated between the Republican State Senate leadership and Governor Mario Cuomo's administration.

This study permits the understanding of many political battles in state politics during the 1990s. It also provides a general understanding of federalism's role in different states and permits the drawing of conclusions about when certain events will be more or less likely to occur in state politics. The analysis of four policy areas in eleven states provides a better understanding of how actors in subnational politics view their roles in providing goods to be consumed by their own and neighboring citizens. This work also offers a better understanding of how state legislators respond, individually and collectively, to the structural incentives and constraints as well as the politics introduced by federalism.

Appendix A

Methodology

I employ case studies and elite interviewing as my principal methods in this research. In this appendix I outline the process by which I selected states for case studies and legislators for interviews. I discuss potential pitfalls common to case-study research and elite interviewing and how I safeguarded against such problems or attempted to mitigate them.

I first selected states for case studies. I defined the eligible population of states as any state that had considered a tax change in 1992, 1993, or 1994. This criterion offered a possible nineteen states from which to sample legislators. From this initial population, I stratified the states according to whether the tax proposal succeeded or failed and then according to various characteristics of its legislature. What was the outcome of the proposal? Did a tax change occur? I selected several states in which legislatures and citizens enacted tax changes and others where the tax proposals failed. I then selected the states based on variations in possible independent variables. I stratified states by population, region, whether they had an income tax, and by partisan control of both houses of the legislature and the governorship. I initially selected nine states based on variation in these factors and then added Vermont and Oregon when additional funding became available in 1994.[1]

One criticism of case studies is that they involve selecting cases purposively (King, Keohane, and Verba 1994). I defend this approach on both methodological and practical grounds. Had I selected states randomly, I might have encountered little or no variation in policy outcomes and thus weakened my ability to explain why some policy proposals succeeded and others did not. Also, I selected states based on variation in both the policy outcome and in potential independent influences on the policy process, such as party control and current tax structure.

After selecting states, I chose state representatives and requested interviews using a random sample. In each state I requested between fifteen and eighteen interviews and conducted between eight and fifteen interviews. I spent four or five days in each state, during which time I interviewed and assembled as much documentation as possible.

Although I randomly selected legislators, they do not represent a random sample of U.S. state lawmakers. They represent eleven random samples of eleven state houses of representatives. The sampling method provided for a representative sample of representatives within each legislature, which was consistent with gaining knowledge about the first unit of analysis, individual legislators' policy preferences, and the second unit of analysis, the collective decisions of state legislatures. Although a random sample of all legislatures would have allowed for individual responses generalizable to the population of U.S. state representatives, it would have been inconsistent with the goal of understanding the collective decisions of state legislatures. On more practical grounds, such a sampling procedure would have exceeded the scope of the study and been nearly impossible to operationalize.

Where I have summarized responses and presented descriptive statistics about legislators' views, I have done so for two reasons. First, summaries offer an indication of the frequency with which different topics were discussed in different states and of the issues with which legislators associated various principles and concepts. Second, these frequencies offer some corroborative evidence that the issues emerging in one state were not idiosyncratic.

The interviews lasted between twenty minutes and two hours, and most ranged between thirty-five and forty-five minutes. In some instances, time or the representative's interests dictated that only one or two issues be discussed. I requested a meeting with each representative individually. In some cases, staff members asked if I would like them to be present, and I declined these courtesies. In two interviews, House members requested that their staff members attend the interview. In these cases, I transcribed only the members' responses and noted staff comments in an addendum.

I did not record the interviews. I developed shorthand and took notes. I then transcribed the interviews as soon after the interview as possible, in most cases within twenty-four hours. In the few cases where I could not transcribe interviews within twenty-four hours, I rewrote my notes, adding details and direct comments, and transcribed them shortly thereafter. I also fleshed out my notes immediately following most interviews.

I typically began with questions about tax policies and economic development and then moved to specific tax proposals, Medicaid spending, education funding, and government mandates. Depending on the state and legislator, the order of questions varied. I began with general questions to afford members an opportunity to volunteer specific ideas and concepts without prompting. If they alluded to a subject or principle, I would insert a question or clarification to gain specificity. If this second question evoked an equally general response, I then asked about a specific idea or piece of legislation. In these cases, I took care to have enough background on the state's political landscape to be able to relate an idea from

TABLE A1. Interview Schedule

Taxes

Did you take a public position on the recent tax proposal?
Personally, what would you like to see happen regarding that proposal? Why?
Opponents (Proponents) of the proposal suggest this scenario. How do you respond?

Economic Development

Personally, what policies and priorities do you have for economic development?
The governor (or House leadership) has offered Proposal X; have you taken a public position on this proposal?

Health Care

Like most states, your state has had to contend with escalating Medicaid costs. What do you think the current legislature might do?
What would you personally like to do with respect to Medicaid specifically? With respect to health care in general?

Education

Have you taken a position on the current proposal? Why?

Government Mandates

The press has recently given attention to the issue of government mandates. In your experience as a legislator, have you encountered any particularly significant mandates?
How have they affected the overall operation of the state government? What benefits can you perceive? What are the problems?
In addition to federal mandates on states, states often mandate that localities comply with regulations or offer services. Are there any local mandates with which you have experience?

a local politician rather than my own.[2] Table A1 presents the basic interview schedule.

Conducting personal interviews offers several advantages over other possible methods of investigating state politics. An alternative would have been to conduct a mail survey of legislators in various states. I rejected this method because conducting the interviews allowed me to garner richer information. Personal interviews allowed me to tailor questions to the specific policy alternatives and politics in each state. The interviews also afforded me the opportunity to explore specific issues in depth with particular legislators. Such explorations would not have been possible using a survey.

Any difficulties in believing legislators in interviews would not be alleviated by using surveys. Indeed, the internal validity and reliability of a survey could be more problematic because one could not verify that the responses were indeed those of a legislator rather than of staff members or associates.

The case-study method allowed me to explore aspects of state politics that deserve greater attention. Many superb models of state politics rely mostly on aggregate or per capita spending and tax data (Garand 1988; Erikson, Wright, and McIver 1993; Dye 1990). These models typically discuss influences on state politics after the fact—that is, after appropriations have been made. Case studies allowed me to witness the policy process at various stages and to gather information about policy alternatives and political strategies leading to policy outcomes that are not revealed by various measures of spending and taxation. My results do not invalidate these other models. Rather, the case studies complement other methods.

An issue that may arise with interviews is whether an interviewer can believe what political elites relate. I employed three techniques for verifying information. First, newspaper articles, lobbyists' fact sheets, and legislative and administrative reports provided supporting evidence for, if not outright verification of, legislators' versions of events. Second, I often attempted innocuously to run a scenario past a legislator whom I suspected might have an alternative view from the original source. For example, I asked New Jersey Republicans about Democrats' claims that Governor Christine Todd Whitman's tax cut would necessitate local property tax increases. Some suggested that it would, and others explained why it would not. In using this technique, I was careful not to identify any proponent or opponent of an argument. I would place an argument before a legislator and ask them to respond by saying, "I understand your point, but others might contend . . ." Respondents often replied with prefatory comments such as, "That's a political argument from the liberals (conservatives). The truth is . . ." Although the arguments and counterarguments rarely provided an objective "truth," they offered a range in which the truth might lie. In some instances, representatives candidly relayed that they personally favored a policy proposal not supported by their party or their constituents. Legislators admitted these political considerations (i.e., party unity and electoral risks) led them to oppose their most preferred policy proposal.

A third means for checking legislators' accounts and perceptions came from staff, reporters, community and political activists, and lobbyists. I used a "snowball" sampling technique to find relevant interviews, and some occurred quite by chance.[3] I contacted lobbyists and staffers based on the recommendations of legislators. This technique allowed me to check both policy proposals and accounts of events. In some cases, it enabled me to have the same information legislators used in shaping policy. I promised these individuals anonymity, and they offered very detailed information and background. I also protected the legislators' identity. Lobbyists, staff, and activists frequently voluntarily identified leaders on various proposals and issues. From these identifications I could check information proffered by lawmakers.[4]

Although I treated the interviewees as informants rather than as respondents to a mass survey, the consistency and frequency with which certain topics, concepts, and principles appeared led me to code the interviews. Most of the coding centered on the frequency with which legislators discussed the six governing principles with respect to various policy areas (i.e., education, Medicaid, and economic development). I first coded the interviews to determine the overall frequency with which legislators discussed the principles regardless of the issue. Then I coded a subset of interviews for each policy area where the subset was comprised of those legislators who discussed the issue. If I did not discuss an issue with a legislator, the interview was not coded for inclusion in that chapter.

An important element of the case studies was acquiring and evaluating secondary evidence. I attempted to gather as many relevant state documents, interest-group publications, and press accounts as time allowed. In several states I sent for documents and bills after returning from the interviews. In addition to corroborating the information from legislators, this information provided valuable contextual and substantive information to write and document this research.

Notes

Chapter 1

1. One concern that the method does not address is temporal. The timing of this study is limited to the mid-1990s, so I cannot conclude that states will never act to raise income taxes. How well these principles interact and play out over time is a good question that further research may elucidate.

2. This research is not an analysis of public finance or tax incidence (Phares 1980). Footnotes offer technical points that may help readers understand the significance or implications of a policy alternative. The appendixes offer summaries of policies or institutional arrangements that affected the pertinent policies.

Chapter 2

1. I also assume that no change in either spending or taxes implies a change in the economic efficiency of financing government goods and services.

2. In this illustration I focus on trade-offs in spending only to keep the analysis as neat as possible. Governments could decide not to trade public goods and particular benefits but could instead choose to cut taxes and thus increase citizens' private incomes.

Chapter 3

1. In Mississippi, the legislature in 1992 established contingency trust funds for education and a general fund to offset future revenue swings resulting from the state's reliance on gambling revenues.

2. For example, New York and New Jersey have agreements regarding the tax treatment of New Jersey residents who work in New York City, and Pennsylvania and New Jersey have agreements about New Jersey residents who work in Philadelphia.

3. Previous work on state politics has largely ignored the influence of symbolic politics. One notable exception is Lowery and Sigelman (1981), which tests the strength of various econometric models designed to explain tax revolts. The

authors conclude that the relative weaknesses of these more conventional models resulted in part from their failure to incorporate measures of symbolic politics. My research offers positive evidence that conforms to Lowery and Sigelman's conclusions.

Chapter 4

1. There has also been a great deal of activity centered on property tax reductions and limitations. I consider these changes in chapter 5 and concentrate on income and sales taxes in this chapter.

2. Much of the increase in state taxes during the 1970s resulted from states assuming greater financial responsibility for local programs, particularly education. Overall, 20 percent of local expenditures shifted to state government between 1960 and 1985.

3. Among states considering income tax reductions are Arizona, Connecticut, New York, New Jersey, Massachusetts, and Montana.

4. In Washington, state and local taxes consume 17.3 percent of the incomes of the poorest fifth of all citizens in the state. Florida and Tennessee also rank among the top ten states in terms of the tax burden placed on low-income citizens.

5. In both New Jersey and Michigan, court order or the threat of litigation motivated some legislators to support major tax changes.

6. The increase in the personal exemption would have been fully offset by the higher tax rate with seven thousand dollars in taxable income. Thus, single people would have received no benefit from the personal-exemption change if their gross annual incomes exceeded ten thousand dollars. The exemption reduction/rate increase would have been tax neutral for a family of four with a gross annual income of forty thousand dollars.

Chapter 5

1. Because both education and infrastructure spending can have characteristics of public goods yet confer particular benefits, many legislators argued for a mixed strategy for providing such goods. They suggested that the appropriate strategy was to have citizens pay according for a portion of individual benefits they might receive from a program but to have the state pay from its general revenues for the portion of benefits likely to accrue to the state. For example, in an education program, the state could subsidize tuition at a technical vocational school and yet require some tuition from students, who would benefit from higher wages in the future. In the case of infrastructure spending, the state could initially finance road construction but then apply a gas tax or toll to recoup its investment from those most particularly benefiting from new roads.

2. Jackson and Hawthorne (1987) and Jackson and King (1989) argue that the tax incidence generates a particular income distribution that in turn can be considered a collective good within a polity.

3. The same legislator hoped that there would be positive spin-off effects from Mercedes's new plant in Alabama. He suggested that since his district was near the

border, he hoped Mercedes's suppliers would locate across the border in Mississippi. The representative readily conceded that such a scenario was preferable to having to forgo Mississippi revenues to attract the initial or anchor business (i.e., Mercedes).

4. Literature from the State Department for Economic Development confirmed that more than 60 percent of the geographic area of Colorado was covered by various enterprise zones.

5. At least one legislator in every case-study state except Massachusetts mentioned the tax incentive package that Alabama offered Mercedes in a successful bid to have Mercedes locate its North American plant there. With only two exceptions, legislators felt that Alabama had offered an excessively generous package of incentives. The majority perceived that foregone revenues coupled with marginal expenditures for new services and infrastructure would outweigh marginal revenue benefits attributable to the plant.

6. Legislators cited environmental, health, and workplace safety regulations as most burdensome to employers.

7. The overall number of legislators' preferences shown in table 9 is less than that of table 8 simply because fewer legislators identified a specific second economic-development priority.

8. The schedule for bond assessment fees was 2 percent of an employee's salary for wages between five and seven dollars an hour, 4 percent for wages between seven and nine dollars an hour, and 6 percent for wages over nine dollars an hour.

9. Further exacerbating this situation are the relatively low tax rates on personal income in Mississippi. In all cases, the effective marginal tax rates were lower than employees would pay in debt-service assessments.

10. The initiative limited the rate of growth in state spending to the combined rates of inflation and population growth.

Chapter 6

1. Among the "unfunded" mandates legislators most derided were federal court orders requiring districts to pay for full and equal special education for students with various handicaps or special needs. Although many legislators admired the goal, they felt the individual costs of special education—up to eight times that of the average per-pupil cost—were disproportionate and forced school districts to divert money from programs with broader benefits. Fifteen percent of the legislators interviewed cited special education as the most onerous federal mandate on state government.

2. It would be fair to say that the issue of property taxation as a source of tax rebellion had just emerged at the time of Peterson's analysis, with California's infamous Proposition 13 having appeared on the ballot in 1978.

3. In the well-known case of Kalkaska, Michigan, where the superintendent closed the schools in March 1993 because voters rejected millage increases necessary to fund schools, the district spent $3,800 per pupil in the 1994–95 school year.

4. A similar situation has begun in Colorado, where voters enacted Amendment 1, capping government spending, and subjected all tax increases to popular

votes at the same time they rejected a one cent increase in the sales tax. Colorado legislators expressed concerns that when millage increases were rejected, school districts would turn to the state for relief but the state government would not have the latitude to bail out the localities.

5. The term *backfilling* is used even in official documents in Oregon. If general revenues for a specific program are at their maximum and the expenditure cannot be reduced, the remaining portion of its appropriation must be backfilled. Typically, the legislature has relied on lottery revenues to backfill its budgets.

6. Oregon is one of five states with no sales tax.

7. One proposal designed to control costs was the initiation of a statewide teachers' contract in which the legislature would create a single salary schedule and regulate future raises.

8. One of Vermont's programs provided income tax credits to citizens whose property tax bills exceeded 5 percent of their income.

9. Governor Florio and assembly Republicans financed the initial sales tax reductions with replacement revenue from the state pension fund. They agreed to accounting changes in the valuation of the fund, which created an $800 million surplus in the account. Noting the "excess deposits," Governor Florio ordered $769 million withdrawn to cover the revenue loss from the sales tax rate reduction for the first year and a half of the change. As of 1995, the federal Internal Revenue Service was considering action against the state for this change since the IRS considered the $769 million to have originally been a nontaxable source of employee income (i.e., pension contributions), and then the state changed its accounting and spent the windfall.

10. In 1990 Governor Florio and the Democrat-controlled legislature raised the state sales tax from 6 to 7 percent and added a 7 percent income tax rate for those making in excess of fifty thousand dollars per year.

Chapter 7

1. Legislators justified increased tobacco and alcohol taxes on the grounds that citizens who engaged in those activities would demand more state services later in their lives and therefore deserved to pay taxes to fund health programs.

2. Fifteen Republican legislators noted that they would have difficulty funding increases for anticrime and corrections programs in the absence of Medicaid cost containment.

3. In contrast, 21 percent of representatives cited ballot initiatives as the most constraining or costly mandates, whereas 15 to 17 percent of legislators identified environmental regulations or special-education mandates as the most onerous.

4. Legislators in New Jersey, Michigan, and New York noted that their states offered benefits beyond those required by the federal government. They suggested that they would cut those ancillary benefits prior to attempting any reform efforts.

5. The states' particular health systems to some extent influenced the shape of reforms. In Washington and Oregon, extensive HMO systems and networks offered ready-made avenues for shifting Medicaid recipients into managed care. In Tennessee there was no such HMO system, and the state's dominant insurer, Blue

Cross of Tennessee, developed Tenncare in conjunction with the McWherter administration.

6. Nearly a dozen states had come to rely on health-services-assessment taxes by the early 1990s. Among these states, Tennessee was the most dependent on an assessment tax to operate its entire Medicaid program. Medicaid's hospital tax raised $344 million, which the federal government matched with $688 million to provide more than 60 percent of Tennessee's total Medicaid funding. In contrast, New York's services-assessment tax raised $341 million, equally matched by the federal government to provide 7 percent of the funding for that state's total Medicaid spending.

7. Some of the proponents of Initiative 602 stated that they had reservations about the benefits and service provisions in the 1993 health plan but that they supported the underlying financing.

8. Several legislators who spoke on this issue also noted that health care had been eclipsed in the early months of 1994 by crime as the issue most concerning constituents. Given a limited session and the necessity of addressing a state budget and several state constitutional issues and developing a crime package, several legislators suggested that they relegated health to the back burner both because its complexity would yield little political payoff and because other issues had emerged that could either yield a political dividend or yield negative consequences if the legislature failed to address them.

Appendix A

1. I had selected Oregon to be among the original nine case studies, but its legislature only meets in odd-numbered years. I replaced Oregon with Colorado, which had an identical profile in terms of partisan control of its political institutions, its geography, and its population. Voters in Colorado rejected a 1992 sales tax increase. In 1993 Oregon voters rejected the enactment of a 5 percent sales tax. In the end, Colorado provided more information regarding health-care reform, and Oregon was critical in my research on education finance.

2. The Nexis service at the University of Michigan was invaluable in enabling me to prepare background on each state. The service provided newspaper reviews for every state except Vermont. For that state, I relied on *Vermont Magazine* and several *New York Times* articles from 1992 through 1995.

3. In one case, I conducted a forty-five-minute interview with a lobbyist in Florida while we both waited for a representative who was running behind schedule.

4. In Mississippi, the House sergeant at arms graciously provided me space in which to work in the same general location as the lobbyists' corridor. Several lobbyists included me in their weekly Friday luncheon, which commenced immediately after the House recessed at noon and ended after dinner. This was an excellent format for garnering information.

References

Applebome, Peter. 1994. "Amid Cries of Politicking, a Widely Endorsed Plan Dies." *New York Times,* June 26.

Ballard, Charles, and Don Fullerton. 1992. "Distortionary Taxes and the Provision of Public Goods." *Journal of Economic Perspectives* 6:117–31.

Barancik, Scott, and Isaac Shapiro. 1992. *Where Have All The Dollars Gone? A State-by-State Analysis of Income Disparities over the 1980s.* Washington, DC: Center on Budget and Policy Priorities.

Berry, Frances Stokes, and William D. Berry. 1992. "Tax Innovation in the States: Capitalizing on Political Opportunity." *American Journal of Political Science* 36:715–42.

Beyle, Thad. 1983. *Being Governor: The View from the Office.* Durham, NC: Duke University Press.

Brace, Paul. 1991. "The Changing Context of State Political Economy." *Journal of Politics* 53:297–317.

Brace, Paul. 1993. *State Government and Economic Performance.* Baltimore: Johns Hopkins University Press.

Brown, Lawrence D., James W. Fossett, and Kenneth T. Palmer. 1984. *The Changing Politics of Federal Grants.* Washington, DC: Brookings Institution.

Buchanan, James M. 1968. *The Demand and Supply of Public Goods.* Chicago: Rand McNally.

Burns, Nancy E. 1994. *The Formation of Local Governments: Private Values in Public Institutions.* New York: Oxford University Press.

Celis, William. 1994. "Michigan Votes for Revolution in Financing Its Public Schools." *New York Times,* March 17.

Christoff, Chris. 1994. "Ballot Plan Has the Edge, Polls Show." *Detroit News,* February 19.

Chubb, John. 1985. "The Political Economy of Federalism." *American Political Science Review* 79:994–1015.

Condiff, Michael. 1993. "Economic Development Act Creates Surge of Interest." *Mississippi Business Journal,* July 19.

Conlan, Timothy. 1988. *New Federalism: Intergovernmental Reform and Political Change from Nixon to Reagan.* Washington, DC: Brookings Institution.

169

Council of State Governments. 1994. *The Book of the States.* Vol. 30. Lexington, KY: Council of State Governments.

Courant, Paul N. 1994. "How Would You Know a Good Economic Development Policy If You Tripped Over One? Hint: Don't Just Count Jobs." *National Tax Journal* 47:863–81.

Courant, Paul N., and Edward M. Gramlich. 1991. "The Impact of the Tax Reform Act of 1986 on State and Local Fiscal Behavior." In *Do Taxes Matter? The Impact of the Tax Reform Act of 1986,* ed. Joel Slemrod. Cambridge, MA: MIT Press.

Cypher, James M. 1987. "Military Spending: Technical Change, and Economic Growth: A Disguised Form of Industrial Policy?" *Journal of Economic Issues* 21:33–59.

Denzau, Arthur T., and Michael C. Munger. 1986. "Legislators and Interest Groups: How Unorganized Interests Get Represented." *American Political Science Review* 80 (1): 89–106.

Dye, Thomas. 1990. *American Federalism: Competition among Governments.* Lexington, MA: Lexington Books.

Edelman, Murray J. 1964. *The Symbolic Uses of Politics.* Urbana: University of Illinois Press.

Eisinger, Peter K. 1988. *The Rise of the Entrepreneurial State: State and Local Economic Development Policy in the United States.* Madison: University of Wisconsin Press.

Engler, John. 1994. "Ballot Plan the Right Plan for Workers and Their Families." *Detroit News,* March 9.

Erikson, Robert S., Gerald C. Wright Jr., and John P. McIver. 1989. "Political Parties, Public Opinion, and State Policy in the United States." *American Political Science Review* 83:729–50.

Erikson, Robert S., Gerald C. Wright, and John P. McIver. 1993. *Statehouse Democracy: Public Opinion and Policy in the American States.* Cambridge and New York: Cambridge University Press.

Fenno, Richard F., Jr. 1973. *Congressmen in Committees.* New York: Little, Brown.

Fenno, Richard F., Jr. 1978. *Home Style: House Members and Their Districts.* Glenview, IL: Scott, Foresman.

Fitzgerald, Joan. 1993. "Political Economy and Urban Development." In *Theories of Local Economic Development: Perspectives from Across the Disciplines,* ed. Richard B. Bingham and Robert Meir. Newbury Park, CA: Sage.

Francis, James. 1988. "The Florida Sales Tax on Services: What Really Went Wrong?" In *The Unfinished Agenda for State Tax Reform,* ed. Steven D. Gold. Denver: National Conference of State Legislatures.

Gallup, George, Jr. 1994. *The Gallup Poll: Public Opinion in 1993.* Wilmington, DE: Scholarly Resources.

Galper, Harvey, and Stephen H. Pollock. 1988. "Models of State Income Tax Reform." In *The Unfinished Agenda for State Tax Reform,* ed. Steven D. Gold. Denver: National Conference of State Legislatures.

Garand, James C. 1988. "Explaining Government Growth in the U.S. States." *American Political Science Review* 82:837–49.

Gerber, Elisabeth R. 1996. "Legislative Response to the Threat of Popular Initiatives." *American Journal of Political Science* 40 (1): 99–127.

Gold, Steven D. 1982. "Federal Aid and State Finances." *National Tax Journal* 35:373–82.

Gold, Steven. 1986. *Reforming State Tax Systems.* Denver: National Conference of State Legislatures.

Gold, Steven. 1988. *The Unfinished Agenda for State Tax Reform.* Denver: National Conference of State Legislatures.

Gold, Steven. 1990. *The State Fiscal Agenda for the 1990s.* Denver: National Conference of State Legislatures.

Gold, Steven. 1992. *Public School Finance Programs of the United States and Canada.* Albany: Nelson A. Rockefeller Institute of Government, State University of New York.

Gramlich, Edward M. 1990. *A Guide to Benefit-Cost Analysis.* 2d ed. Englewood Cliffs, NJ: Prentice-Hall.

Green, Donald P., Daniel Kahneman, and Howard Kunreuther. 1994. "How the Scope and Method of Public Funding Affect Willingness to Pay for Public Goods." *Public Opinion Quarterly* 58:49–67.

Hansen, Susan B. 1983. *The Politics of Taxation: Revenue without Representation.* New York: Praeger.

Hanson, Russell. 1994. "Health-Care Reform, Managed Competition, and Subnational Politics." *Publius* 24:49–68.

Holyfield, Jeff. 1994. "Political Fallout from Proposal A Continues Raining Down." *Ann Arbor News,* March 21.

Hornbeck, Mark, and Charlie Cain. 1994. "Voters Overwhelmingly Back Sales Tax Increase." *Detroit News,* March 17.

Jackson, John E., and Michael R. Hawthorne. 1987. "The Individual Political Economy of Federal Tax Policy." *American Political Science Review* 81: 757–74.

Jackson John E., and David King. 1989. "Public Goods, Private Interests, and Representation." *American Political Science Review* 86:1143–64.

Jackson, John E., and John W. Kingdon. 1992. "Ideology, Interest Group Scores, and Legislative Votes." *American Journal of Political Science* 36 (3): 805–23.

Jewell, Malcolm. 1982. *Representation in State Legislatures.* Lexington: University of Kentucky Press.

Kenyon, Daphne. 1991. *Interjurisdictional Tax Policy Competition: Good or Bad for the Federal System?* Washington, DC: Advisory Commission on Intergovernmental Relations.

Key, V. O. 1949. *Southern Politics in State and Nation.* New York: Knopf.

Key, V. O. 1956. *American State Politics: An Introduction.* New York: Knopf.

King, Gary, Robert O. Keohane, and Sidney Verba. 1994. *Designing Social Inquiry.* Princeton: Princeton University Press.

Kingdon, John. 1989. *Congressmen's Voting Decisions.* 3d ed. Ann Arbor: University of Michigan Press.

Kingdon, John. 1990. *Agendas, Alternatives, and Public Policies.* New York: HarperCollins.

Konda, Thomas, James C. Garand, and David Lowery. 1984. "Spending in the States: A Test of Six Models." *Western Political Quarterly* 37:48–66.

Krehbiel, Keith. 1991. *Information and Legislative Organization.* Ann Arbor: University of Michigan Press.

Laver, Michael. 1981. *The Politics of Private Desires.* New York: Penguin.

Leff, Mark Hugh. 1984. *The Limits of Symbolic Reform: The New Deal and Taxation, 1933–1939.* New York: Cambridge University Press.

Leib, Jeffrey. 1992. "Tax Law Dims Chances for Pentagon Center." *Denver Post,* December 24.

Leib, Jeffrey. 1993. "Rewritten Ziff Bill in Works." *Denver Post,* April 23.

Levi, Margaret. 1987. *Of Rule and Revenue.* Berkeley and Los Angeles: University of California Press.

Levin, Henry M. 1987. "Education as a Public and Private Good." *Journal of Policy Analysis and Management* 6:628–41.

Lilley, William, III, Laurence J. DeFranco, and William M. Diefenderfer III. 1993. *State Data Atlas: The Almanac of State Legislatures.* Washington, DC: Congressional Quarterly.

Lindblom, Charles. 1993. *The Policy-making Process.* Englewood Cliffs, NJ: Prentice-Hall.

Lowery, David, and Lee Sigelman. 1981. "Understanding the Tax Revolt: Eight Explanations." *American Political Science Review* 75:963–74.

Mas-Colell, Andreu, and Joaquim Silvestre. 1989. "Cost-Share Equilibria: A Lindahlian Approach." *Journal of Economic Theory* 47:239–56.

Mayhew, David. 1974. *Congress: The Electoral Connection.* New Haven: Yale University Press.

McIntyre, Robert S., Douglas P. Kelly, Michael P. Ettinger, and Elizabeth A. Fray. 1991. *A Far Cry from Fair: CTJ's Guide to State Tax Reform.* Washington, DC: Citizens for Tax Justice.

Meltsner, Arnold J. 1971. *The Politics of City Revenue.* Berkeley: University of California Press.

Mintz, Alex, and Chi Huang. 1990. "Defense Expenditures, Economic Growth, and the 'Peace Dividend.'" *American Political Science Review* 84:1283–93.

Mississippi, State of. 1994. *Proposed Budget.* Submitted by Governor Kirk Fordice and Joint Legislative Committee. Jackson, MS.

Oates, Wallace. 1972. *Fiscal Federalism.* New York: Harcourt, Brace, Jovanovich.

Oregon Health Services Commission, Office of Health Policy, Department of Human Resources. 1994. *Prioritization of Health Services: A Report to the Governor and Legislature.* Salem, OR.

Oregon Legislative Revenue Office. 1995a. *Basic Tax Packet.* Salem, OR.

Oregon Legislative Revenue Office. 1995b. *Impact of Measure 1.* Research Report 3–93. Salem, OR.

Padgett, John. 1978. "Bounded Rationality in the Budgetary Process." *American Political Science Review* 72:354–72.

Pauly, Mark, and Thomas W. Granneman. 1983. *Controlling Medicaid Costs: Fed-*

eralism, Competition, and Choice. Washington, DC: American Enterprise Institute for Policy Research.

Pear, Robert. 1994a. "States Again Try Health Changes as Congress Fails." *New York Times,* September 16.

Pear, Robert. 1994b. "Vermont Shows Way a Health Bill Can Fail." *New York Times,* June 8.

Peterson, Paul. 1981. *City Limits.* Chicago: University of Chicago Press.

Peterson, Paul, and Mark Rom. 1990. *Welfare Magnets: A New Case for a National Standard.* Washington, DC: Brookings Institution.

Phares, Donald. 1980. *Who Pays State and Local Taxes?* Cambridge, MA: Oelgeschlager, Gunn, and Hann.

Pitkin, Hanna Fenichel. 1967. *The Concept of Representation.* Berkeley: University of California Press.

Plotnick, Robert, and Richard Winters. 1985. "A Politico-Economic Theory of Income Redistribution." *American Political Science Review* 79:458–73.

Poterba, James M. 1994. "State Responses to Fiscal Crises: The Effects of Budgetary Institutions and Politics." *Journal of Political Economy* 102:799–821.

Riker, William H. 1987. *The Development of American Federalism.* Boston: Kluwer Academic Publishers.

Roberts, Russell D. 1987. "Financing Public Goods." *Journal of Political Economy* 95:420–37.

Samuelson, Paul A. 1954. "The Pure Theory of Public Expenditure." *Review of Economics and Statistics* 36:387–89.

Savage, James D. 1988. *Balanced Budgets and American Politics.* Ithaca: Cornell University Press.

Schulman, Bruce. 1992. *From Cotton Belt to Sunbelt: Federal Policy, Economic Development, and the Transformation of the South.* New York: Oxford University Press.

Steuerle, C. Eugene. 1991. *The Tax Decade: How Taxes Came to Dominate the Public Agenda.* Washington, DC: Urban Institute Press.

Tennessee, State of. *Budget Supplement.* 1994–95. Nashville: Department of Finance and Administration.

Tiebout, Charles M. 1956. "A Pure Theory of Local Government Expenditures." *Journal of Political Economy* 44:416–24.

U.S. Advisory Commission on Intergovernmental Relations. 1991. *Competition among States and Local Governments: Efficiency and Equity in American Federalism.* Washington, DC: Urban Institute Press.

U.S. Advisory Commission on Intergovernmental Relations. 1992. *Medicaid: Intergovernmental Trends and Options.* Washington, DC: Advisory Commission on Intergovernmental Relations.

U.S. Advisory Commission on Intergovernmental Relations. 1993. *Federal Regulation of State and Local Governments: The Mixed Record of the 1980s.* Washington, DC: Advisory Commission on Intergovernmental Relations.

U.S. Bureau of the Census. 1993. *Government Finances, 1991–1992.* Washington, DC: Department of Commerce.

U.S. Department of Education. 1992. *Digest of Education Statistics.* Washington, DC: Government Printing Office.

U.S. House of Representatives, Committee on Ways and Means. 1992. *1992 Green Book: Background Material and Data on Programs within the Jurisdiction of the Committee on Ways and Means.* Washington DC: Government Printing Office.

Van Son, Victoria. 1993. *CQ's State Fact Finder: Rankings across America.* Washington, DC: Congressional Quarterly.

Vermont, State of. 1995. *Budget for Fiscal Year 1996.* Montpelier, VT.

Vermont House of Representatives. 1995. *H. 351: Taxation, Education Finance.* Montpelier, VT.

Walker, Jack L. 1969. "The Diffusion of Innovations among the American States." *American Political Science Review* 66:880–99.

Walsh, Annmarie Hauck. 1978. *The Public's Business: The Politics and Practices of Government Corporations.* Cambridge: MIT Press.

Young, Linda. 1993. "Meridian Base Closing Would Be Like Shutting Down a Small City." *Mississippi Business Journal,* April 12.

Index